THE WAY OF THE FOOL

How to Stop Worrying
About Life and Start Living It...
in 12½ Super-Simple Steps!

Mark David Gerson

The Way of the Fool: How to Stop Worrying About
Life and Start Living It…in 12½ Super Simple Steps!

Copyright © 2018, 2019 Mark David Gerson
All rights reserved

No part of this book may be reproduced, stored in a retrieval system
or transmitted by any means, electronic, mechanical, photocopying,
recording or otherwise, without written permission from the author,
except for the inclusion of brief quotations in critical reviews and
certain other noncommercial uses permitted by copyright law.

First Edition 2018. Second Edition 2019.

Published by MDG Media International
2370 W. State Route 89a, Suite 11-210
Sedona, AZ 86336

www.mdgmediainternational.com

ISBN: 978-1-950189-15-1

Author Photograph: Kevin Truong
www.kevintruong.com

More information
www.markdavidgerson.com

*"You either trust or you do not.
There is no halfway in between."*
THE MOONQUEST

"What, me worry?"
ALFRED E. NEUMAN, *MAD* MAGAZINE

To my mother, whose Fool-ish leap of faith
gave me life.

Praise for The Fool

The Way of the Fool
The Way of the Imperfect Fool
The Way of the Abundant Fool
The Way of the Creative Fool

It will transform your life! Don't just read it. Live it!
Rev. Brendalyn Batchelor – Unity Santa Fe

Making any life-changing decision takes courage and support. This book has afforded me both.
Isa de Quesada – Tillamook, OR

Simple but powerful!
Dave Kerpen – author of "The Art of People"

Inspired and inspiring… A powerful but accessible guide.
Dan Stone – author of "Ice on Fire"

A must-read guidebook to living your richest, most authentic life!
Joan Cerio – author of "Heartwired to Heaven"

Lays the groundwork for you to step out of your own way and pursue your dreams… A book that changes everything that's holding you back!
Ted Wiga – San Francisco, CA

More from Mark David Gerson

Self-Help & Personal Growth

The Book of Messages: Writings Inspired by Melchizedek

Memoir

Acts of Surrender: A Writer's Memoir
Dialogues with the Divine: Encounters with my Wisest Self
Pilgrimage: A Fool's Journey
All That Matters Is That I'm Writing: A Writer's Journey

Fiction

The MoonQuest
The StarQuest
The SunQuest
The Bard of Bryn Doon
The Lost Horse of Bryn Doon
The Sorcerer of Bryn Doon
Sara's Year
After Sara's Year
The Emmeline Papers

For Writers & Aspiring Writers

The Voice of the Muse: Answering the Call to Write
The Voice of the Muse Companion: Guided Meditations for Writers
From Memory to Memoir: Writing the Stories of Your Life
Organic Screenwriting: Writing for Film, Naturally
Birthing Your Book…Even If You Don't Know What It's About
The Heartful Art of Revision: An Intuitive Guide to Editing
Writer's Block Unblocked: Seven Surefire Ways to Free Up Your Writing and Creative Flow
Time to Write
Write with Ease
Free Your Characters, Free Your Story
Write to Heal
Journal from the Heart

Contents

Introduction	9
Getting Started	11
The Steps	17
Step #1. Break Free	21
Step #2. Be In the Moment	33
Step #3. Follow Your Heart	47
Step #4. Love Yourself, Love Your Path	63
Step #5. Be Vulnerable	79
Step #6. Let Go	95
Step #7. Take Risks	109
Step #8. Live Your Passion	121
Step #9. Don't Give Up	135
Step #10. Embrace the Mystery	147
Step #11. Embrace the Magic	157
Step #12. Remember Who You Are	169
Step #12½. Fly Free	179
The Way of the Fool and You	189
Afterword: The Fool and I	191
Gratitude	193

Introduction

YOU HAVE ONLY TO look at the ever-expanding catalog of stress-related symptoms (a Google search yields nearly a million results) and stress-relief solutions (ten million Google results) to recognize that we are, literally, plagued with worry.

On top of the normal strain and anxiety of our everyday lives — health, school, jobs, families, finances, relationships — we are bombarded nonstop with the cacophony of news, information, analysis and chatter that our electronic devices hurl at us. We can know what's going on everywhere the instant it is happening, be it down the street or on the other side of the planet...even as we have fewer and fewer ways to distinguish whether what's coming at us is fact or fiction. Put it all together and the intellectual and emotional overload can be overwhelming. Some days it can be paralyzing.

So why apply a centuries-old concept to a twenty-first century problem? Because the Fool is more than the first card of a tarot deck. It's more than a game piece or metaphysical divination device. It's an archetype, a sort of mythic character that lives inside us — inside the collective unconscious of all humanity. And like all archetypes, it speaks to our very essence as human beings...to an aspect of our consciousness that not only evokes powerful emotions and reveals who we are at our deepest levels but that can offer powerful tools for living that are available to all of us.

The archetype of the Fool offers a particularly potent set of tools to help us deal with the intensity of these times. How? By showing us how we can minimize worry and maximize joy, how we can dissolve the blocks that hold us back from accessing and experiencing our passion, how we can take those leaps of faith that free us to soar into our heart's desire.

The 12½ steps of *The Way of the Fool* are designed to do all that and more — simply and effectively. If stress is making you sick and anxiety is wearing you down, if the pressures of daily life have hijacked your dreams, *The Way of the Fool* is your fast-track to a renewed sense of purpose and zest for life.

The best news of all is that none of these steps is difficult to implement. Of course not. Why would the Fool walk a complex, complicated path?

Nor is the Way of the Fool likely to be entirely alien to you. There's a good chance that you will recognize at least a few of its 12½ steps. The fact is, none of them is radical or new. How can they be when they're built on an archetype that already lives as a potential within each of us?

Here's what is revolutionary and groundbreaking: distilling the age-old wisdom of the Fool into a clear, step-by-step guide — a guide to living a fuller, more authentic life…the life *you* were meant to live.

The next chapter will offer you some tips and best practices for using *The Way of the Fool*. It will also answer the most burning question many of you first had when you saw the book's subtitle: "Why twelve and a *half* steps? Why not thirteen?"

So what are you waiting for? Turn the page and join me for the journey of a lifetime on the Way of the Fool!

Getting Started

I WOULD HARDLY BE true to the spirit of the Fool if I were to insist that you follow the 12½ steps outlined here precisely as presented. After all, if the Fool is about anything, it's about finding your own way *in* your own way. Having said that, the journey set out in *The Way of the Fool* follows a certain, dare I say it, logical progression that I would invite you to at least consider. I would especially urge you to consider starting with Step #1 and completing your Fool's journey with Step #12½, regardless of what you do in between. Still, if you feel otherwise inclined, go for it!

Each of the 12½ steps consists of several elements:

- Stories, mine and/or others', that demonstrate the step in action
- Stories that link the step to the archetype of the Fool
- Practical tips and powerful exercises to help you experience the step and integrate it into your day
- A simple affirmation to help anchor that step into your life

Just as there is no prescribed way to move through the steps, there is also no optimal amount of time for you to spend on each step. Everyone is different, and everyone comes to this process from a unique history and set of experiences. Use your discernment to stay with each step until you feel a subtle or not so subtle shift in consciousness and awareness. And as issues come up for you, either while working with *The Way of the Fool* or after you have completed it, feel free to repeat any step or exercise that feels particularly relevant. As for the affirmations, they are designed to be used daily or as often as you feel the need.

Your "Way of the Fool" Journal

I strongly suggest that you start a *Way of the Fool* journal as a companion to your work with this book. Use it, of course, for the exercises and explorations included with each of the 12½ steps. Use it as well as for any other *Way of the Fool*-related experiences you choose to probe or chronicle.

Your *Way of the Fool* journal can be a dedicated journal or you can integrate it into an existing journal. It can be a physical book or a journal that you keep on your computer, tablet or smartphone, either using your device's regular writing software or one of the many journaling apps available for your operating system. If you're more comfortable audio- or video-recording your thoughts and impressions, it would be a good idea to store those files in a *Way of the Fool* folder for easier access.

Regardless, have your *Way of the Fool* journal handy each time you work with the book.

Guided Meditations

The Way of the Fool includes a series of guided meditations and meditative journeys to help you work with many of the book's 12½ steps. When doing any of the meditations, always have easy access to your *Way of the Fool* journal so that you can record your thoughts, feelings and impressions.

How to Use the Meditations:

- Record them yourself for playback.
- Have a friend read them to you, then return the favor.
- Get into a quiet space and place, program your music player for five to forty minutes of contemplative music or nature sounds (depending on the length of the exercise) and read the meditation slowly and receptively, following its directions and suggestions.

If you prefer a professionally guided approach, I have recorded three of this book's meditations on *The Voice of the Muse Companion: Guided Meditations for Writers*. Although my recordings are aimed at writers, they are nearly identical to the versions scripted in this book:

- "Listen to Your Heart" — Step #3 (the recorded version is titled "Write from the Heart")
- "Taming Your Inner Critic" — Step #4
- "The Butterfly" — Step #12½

How to Access the Three Recordings…

- Stream the tracks for free as a subscriber to Apple Music, YouTube Music or Amazon's Music Unlimited.
- Download the individual tracks from Amazon or Apple Music.
- Download the complete album from my website (www.markdavidgerson.com/books), Apple Music, Amazon or CD Baby.

What's a "Muse Stream"

As several of the journaling exercises in *The Way of the Fool* suggest that you write on what I call the "Muse Stream," I figured that I had better explain what it is!

If you're familiar with terms like "free writing," "automatic writing," "stream-of-consciousness writing" or "morning pages" or if you have read any of my books for writers, then you already have a sense of what the Muse Stream is about: a wholesale, uncensored, right-brain outpouring onto the page. It's a practical tool that can get you past your inner critic, inner censor, analytical mind and second thoughts to that place where your truest, most authentic reflections and feelings reside. The key to the Muse Stream is to write without stopping. Without stopping to think…without stopping to stress or to worry.

That's the ideal. But as you'll learn in Step #4, perfection isn't possible. So what happens when you find yourself stuck? When anxiety or judgment aborts the free flow of your freest expression? When a boulder drops into the middle of your Muse Stream and dams up that outpouring?

Here are a couple of tips:

- **Repetition.** Repeat anything to keep your pen or fingers in motion: the previous word/sentence, your opening word/sentence, or anything at all, even if it's "I don't know what to write" or "This is dumb."

- **Free-association.** Let one word trigger the next — whatever leaps to mind, however silly. Let that word trigger the next and the next and so on…until the flow returns.

- **Nonsense words.** Make up words…words that sound funny…words that sound weird…words that are unpronounceable…words that don't exist in any

language or dictionary. Make up one, jot it down…
then another…then another…then another. This
playful act tricks your inner censor into dropping its
guard. Soon, nonsense words will turn into familiar
words and your Muse Stream flow will resume.

- **BREATH.** The best way to remain present and in the
flow is through your breath. Write "I am breathing
in" as you inhale, "I am breathing out" as you
exhale. Keep doing that until the flow returns.

The bottom line: Do *anything* to keep words flowing onto your page!

Celebrate!

I don't know whether it's human nature to focus on what we haven't accomplished and to ignore or belittle our achievements, or whether we have been educated and socialized to do it. Regardless, we tend to spend much more time on our failures than on our successes.

That practice is not only counterintuitive, it's counterproductive. That's because, as the maxim goes, "energy flows where attention goes." In other words, the more we focus on our success, the more success we attract into our life.

So here's the first thing I want you to do with your *Way of the Fool* journal: Create a daily "success diary."

Each night before you turn in, inventory your day…but ignore any goal unreached and all tasks left undone.

Instead, as you run through your day, acknowledge everything you achieved, however seemingly inconsequential, and note it in your journal. Include your progress on your Fool's journey, of course, but don't limit it to that Include everything.

Continue this inventory for at least as long as you're working with this book. And as the days progress, notice how your focus evolves from your perceived failures and not-good-enoughs toward your real successes and attainments, and not only with *The Way of the Fool*.

Once a week, pick your most outstanding accomplishment and find a way to reward yourself for it. It doesn't have to be an extravagant or expensive reward. It could be a specialty coffee at your favorite café, a book you've long coveted or any meaningful acknowledgment. Whatever your reward, let it be something special. However you earned it, celebrate it!

A Note About Gender

The Fool knows no gender. Unfortunately, the English language wasn't designed for that kind of imprecision. The Fool, of course, was…as you'll see in Step #1. As such, when it comes to pronouns, *The Way of the Fool* alternates between "he" and "she" when referring to the Fool. It seemed the most Fool-ish way to go!

Why 12½ Steps?

I promised an answer, and here it is. Sort of…

Of course, I could have given you thirteen steps instead of 12½. I could even have given you fourteen, given that the chapter titled "Beyond the 12½th Step" is itself a sort of step.

But doesn't 12½ sound, well, more Fool-ish? And being Fool-ish is what this book is all about. So let's get past "Getting Started" and really *get started*!

The Steps

1. Break Free

2. Be In the Moment

3. Follow Your Heart

4. Love Yourself, Love Your Path

5. Be Vulnerable

6. Let Go

7. Take Risks

8. Live Your Passion

9. Don't Give Up

10. Embrace the Mystery

11. Embrace the Magic

12. Remember Who You Are

12½. Fly Free

Step #1. Break Free

"There is no right way. There is no wrong way. There is only your way...the way that works for you, today."

THE VOICE OF THE MUSE:
ANSWERING THE CALL TO WRITE

Living an authentic life — what I like to call a "creative life" — is not about doing things the way they have always been done by everyone else...or even by one someone else, even if that someone is a great master, teacher or guru.

Living an authentic life is about finding your own way, blazing your own trail, forging your own path, breaking new ground. It's about busting through old paradigms so that you can bust free to discover your passion and fulfill your potential.

Living a creative life means there can never be a single right way that works for everyone all the time.

There is no universal wrong way either, only the way that works for you...today. So find *your* way!

My Story

IN 1983 I WAS A MONTREAL-based freelance writer and editor, most of my income derived from my Quebec-correspondent post with *The Chronicle of Higher Education*, a Washington-based trade weekly. I had no awakened spirituality in those days, yet some powerful inner force urged me to leave my hometown and move to Toronto.

There was some conventional logic to the call. As an English-language freelancer in a largely French-speaking milieu, my prospects for professional advancement could only improve in English Canada's cultural and communications capital.

At the same time, it seemed heartless to consider a move at that time. Why? My mother had just been diagnosed with cancer and her prognosis was uncertain. How could I even consider moving away…even a relatively accessible 350 miles away? What kind of son would abandon his mother like that?

Today, buttressed by a quarter of a century of Fool-ish living, I would surrender to the imperative and make the move, however emotionally torn I might feel. With today's awareness, I would also understand why I had to leave: My mother had always been such a dominant force in my life that I had to empower myself to separate from her before she left me by dying. At the time, all I could do was balance guilt and responsibility against a certainty that I neither understood nor dared communicate, while gathering whatever scraps of logic I could to support my case.

First, I called my editor at *The Chronicle* to ask whether I would be able to stay on with the newspaper were I to be based in Toronto. His reply was more than I could have hoped for: "We now need someone to cover the whole country. Would you like to be our Canadian correspondent instead?" My monthly retainer would increase accordingly.

So far, so good.

Next, I made a surreptitious visit to my mother's oncologist. "I know this isn't a fair question," I began awkwardly, "but how long does my mother have?" If he were to answer, "Oh, years," I could leave without guilt. If he were to reveal that her time was short, I could choose to wait her out and delay the move.

The doctor's reply failed to offer me the guilt-free certainty I was seeking. "I can give you a statistic," he said, "but that wouldn't mean anything. Cancer patients in your mother's situation can live five weeks, five months or five years. Or longer. You have to do what's right for you. You have to live your life, not your mother's."

He was right. In the next days, I confirmed my move with *The Chronicle* and broke the news to my mother, who was sad but stoic. Two months later, excited to be embarking on my biggest adventure yet, I was gone, having broken free from what was expected of me to find my own "right way."

The Way of the Fool

Look at any tarot deck, including the classic Rider-Waite version used on the cover of this book, and you'll notice that the Fool is nearly always represented as having embarked on a journey that defies logic. He travels with few or no possessions and has no itinerary, unless you consider stepping of a cliff to be an itinerary. In a world of maps, schedules and timetables, a world programmed by predetermined routes, prearranged modes of travel and preplanned agendas, she has broken free not only of all rules but of "common sense."

The Way of the Fool bucks convention, ignores conventional wisdom and lays down no rigid rules, agendas or canons. The Way of the Fool sets out no unyielding shoulds, musts or have-to's. The Way of the Fool hews inflexibly to no one else's systems, methods or orthodoxies.

The Way of the Fool strips off all straitjackets and sheds all externally imposed expectations. It sheds most internally imposed ones as well.

The Way of the Fool steps off established highways and byways to trail-blaze an exceptional journey that reflects an exceptional heart and soul.

The Way of the Fool is not a single "way" or even a "good way." Nor is it a universal "right way." Rather, it's the way that is the only "*right* way" in that moment.

The Way of the Fool colors outside the lines and crafts a life that is distinctive and authentic. More accurately, the Fool rejects coloring books altogether, preferring the blank canvas of total faith.

Ongoing and unconditional faith *is* the Way of the Fool. When we surrender to it, we free ourselves to discover a path that is uniquely our own — with all its unexpected, sometimes uncomfortable and always rewarding gifts and blessings.

A Fool-ish Story

Jeanne Baret broke free in more than one way when she became the first woman to circumnavigate the globe in the late 1760s. Because the French navy banned women from its ships, Baret and her live-in lover, Philibert Commerçon, who had scored the botanist position on the round-the-world expedition, hatched a daring plan: Jeanne would bind her breasts with linen bandages and disguise herself as a young man for the years-long journey aboard Admiral Louis-Antoine de Bougainville's *Étoile*.

The ruse worked, until the *Étoile* reached the South Pacific. Stories vary as to how Baret was exposed. But when she was, she and Commerçon were forced off the ship.

Although the bougainvillea was named for de Bougainville and more than seventy plant species found by the couple have been named for Commerçon, it would take until 2012 for Baret to be similarly honored.

"I have always admired [botanical] explorers," biologist Eric Tepe explained in honoring Baret with the *Solanum baretiae*, a vegetable related to the tomato and potato. "We know many of their names, and they all have endured hardships in pursuit of interesting plants, but few have sacrificed so much and endured so much as Baret."

Your Story

Your "Way of the Fool" Journal

Have you started your *Way of the Fool* journal yet? If not, do it now, before you read on. Remember, there is no "right" way to answer this book's questions, complete its exercises or keep track of your thoughts and experiences as you explore the 12½ steps on the Way of the Fool.

Whether you keep your *Way of the Fool* journal in writing, as a series of audio or video recordings or in a way that's unique to you, I promise that you will derive great benefit from the experience.

For more journaling tips and suggestions, revisit "Getting Started."

Quick Meditation

This is a great way to start your day. Before getting out of bed in the morning, close your eyes, take a few deep breaths, relax and ask yourself this question: What rule, routine, should, must or expectation can I bust and break free of today?

Let the first answer that bubbles up to your conscious mind be the answer. Take a moment to commit to that, preferably in writing in your *Way of the Fool* journal.

Ask Yourself These Questions...

Ask yourself these questions in your *Way of the Fool*

journal but don't think about the answers. And don't feel as though you must answer each question individually if that doesn't feel right. It's okay to break the rules!

Let your individual answers (or whatever single answer these questions trigger) emerge freely and honestly, writing them on the Muse Stream in a free-flowing, stream-of-consciousness way where appropriate:

- Where in my life am I letting other people's rules, paths and ways of doing things get in the way of discovering my own? Why am I making that choice? Those choices?

- Where am I a follower when I could be an explorer and a trailblazer? How can I make that shift? What steps can I take in that direction today? What one step can I take *right now*?

- Where am I being ruled by others' expectations for me? Whose expectations? Why do I feel attached to those expectations? What steps can I take to detach from at least one expectation? What one step can I take *right now*?

- What can I do, starting today, to better chart my own course in my life?

Exploration

For this exercise you will need lined paper and a pen, pencil, colored marker or other writing implement. Do your best to find lined paper, but it's okay to use unlined paper if you can't. (Doing the exercise on a computer or mobile device will dilute its impact.)

Turn your paper sideways, so that you are writing lengthways. On lined or "ruled" paper, you will be writing "against the rules." Even on unlined paper, you will be going against the established order of things. Be even more unconventional by writing with colored pencils or markers and/or by writing diagonally across the page, in spirals or in some other unordered way.

Make a list of as many of the perceived shoulds/musts/have-to's in your life as you can think of. Next to each, counter it with at least one way that you can break that "rule."

Within the next 24 hours, break at least one of those "rules," then journal about how that felt.

Repeat the exercise, focusing on someone else's expectations of you.

My Story: Coda

My mother rarely pressured me to be or do anything other than what I chose to be or do. Yet as courageous as I had allowed myself to be while she was alive — to come out as a gay man, for example, or to quit a secure job for the risks of freelancing or to leave my hometown — all my choices and actions had inevitably been colored by how I thought she might respond and had been filtered through the world view of a woman most of whose life choices had been circumscribed by fear...of not doing the "right thing," of what neighbors or family members might say, of being judged as inadequate or not good enough.

Once she was gone — she died eight months after I left Montreal — all her hopes, fears and expectations for me were also gone. Suddenly, without being conscious of it or of what it meant, I was free.

It would take me a decade to begin to grow into that freedom, but the seeds were planted the day I decided to buck convention and leave Montreal...the day I decided, however unconsciously, to follow the Way of the Fool.

Affirmation

I, *your full name*, forge my own path, blaze my own trail and make my own way in the world, busting through all perceived shoulds, musts, have-to's and expectations. In joy, faith and surrender, I walk the Way of the Fool. And so it is.

Step #2. Be In the Moment

"There is but this moment and the accumulation of connected moments that, in the end, adds up to a lifetime."
THE EMMELINE PAPERS

If there is no right or wrong way, only the way that works for you today (Step #1), then you might as well live in the present moment. After all, what works for you today may not work tomorrow...or ever again.

The fact is, no moment other than this one truly exists, just as no other breath truly exists other than the one you're now breathing.

So focus on now — on this breath, on this moment, on this experience. Don't worry about tomorrow's or about any of the choices or decisions waiting for you next week or next month or next year.

Trust all future breaths, moments and experiences to take care of themselves...and of you. And they will. Be in this moment...and now this one...and now this one.

Be. Present. *Now.*

My Story

IN LATE 2004 WITH my six-year marriage suddenly over, I took off on an open-ended road odyssey that would turn out to last more than thirty months. During my nearly three years of full-time travel, I crisscrossed the US multiple times, supporting myself through metaphysical/inspirational teleconferences and other events, private energy-healing sessions, spiritual coaching, writing workshops…and random miracles. My credit was still bruised from the beating it had taken a few years earlier while I was living on Maui, and I was operating, somewhat stressfully, on a cash-only basis.

In the early weeks of my journeying, I was so emotionally and financially on edge that it took little to push me into full-blown panic. On one of those days, somewhere on some anonymous state highway, I began to fret. Perhaps fewer people than expected had paid for an upcoming teleconference. Perhaps a hoped-for client had failed to materialize. Perhaps some significant bill was coming due. Whatever the trigger, my heart began to race as I ran columns of figures through my throbbing head.

In the midst of all the anxious self-talk and frenzied calculations, a calm inner voice thrust itself into my awareness with a series of questions.

Is there gas in the tank?
Yes… What was this about?
Do you have money for food for today?
Uh-huh.

Do you have a place to stay tonight or money for a hotel room?

Ye-e-s.

Is there anything that's in immediate danger of being taken away from you because you haven't paid a bill?

I shook my head. Nothing was imminently problematic.

Then focus on today, and let tomorrow take care of itself.

Of course.

I would recall that experience frequently in the months that followed, especially when it came to my car payment, then my single largest monthly expense. Somehow, I managed never to be more than a few days' late with it or with any bill. Somehow, there was always enough money to get me through the day. Somehow, by remaining focused on the present moment, the next moment always took care of itself.

The Way of the Fool

Look at the Fool on the card on the cover. Does he seem worried? Does she appear to be distressed or distraught? Is he casting regretful glances over his shoulder at whatever he left behind, in the past? Is she fearfully eyeing the canyon floor, which could well be her future, or the cliff edge, which could easily crumble and send her plummeting?

No. Both the Fool's face and posture suggest that he is unconcerned with where he has come from and untroubled by where he is going. She stands blissfully in the moment, living *now*. And in that "now moment," our Fool is uncompromisingly alive, savoring all the gifts that are granted only to those who are fully present.

It's no accident that the word "present" simultaneously suggests "existence," "now-time" and "gift." In effect, our presence exists only in the gift of the moment. When we refuse that gift by stepping out of the moment, we also step out of our presence and, in a sense, dilute our very existence.

Each time we worry, we remove ourselves from the present moment — a moment during which the cause of our worry is rarely an immediate threat or concern. Each time we worry, we project ourselves forward into a virtual moment in a future we are desperate to control, a future that may never come to pass.

Each time we censor our words, thoughts or actions for fear of being attacked, condemned or censured, we remove ourselves from the present moment — a moment of truth sacrificed on the altar of potential consequences. Each time we censor our words, thoughts or actions, we deny our presence by denying our heart its voice and our soul its song.

Each time we judge or second-guess ourselves, we remove ourselves from the present moment — a moment in which whatever has triggered our judgment is no longer *present*. Each time we judge or second-guess ourselves, we step back in time, to a moment in a past that not only no longer exists but that can never again be present.

The Way of the Fool is a breath-by-breath, moment-to-moment journey that neither looks back in judgment nor forward in anxiety. Nor does it attach itself to particular outcomes.

The Fool learns from the past, but not from a place of recrimination. The Fool plans and takes action toward the future, but not from a place of fear. The Fool has goals and objectives, but no expectations. Rather, the Fool deals identically with past, present and future: with heartful discernment and in a centered groundedness that is always anchored in the now.

When you walk the Way of the Fool, all you can do is live the truth of this moment, of this feeling, of this breath…then move on to the next and live its truth.

A Fool-ish Story

There's a scene in my fantasy novel *The MoonQuest* where Toshar, the main character, steps onto a translucent road, which is his only route back to earth from a celestial plateau high above the suns (there are two suns in the world of the book).

"I quickly learned," Toshar recounts in the story, "to train my eyes to look no more than a few paces ahead. At that distance, a faint, silvery glow marked out my path. It was almost opaque. Yet if I looked back or farther ahead, I saw no sign of road. No sign of anything."

In Toshar's world, as in yours and mine, the past and future have no substance. Only the present moment exists.

Your Story

Quick Meditation

Stop whatever you're doing, close your eyes and take a deep breathe in and out. Really be with this breath. And now this one. Why would you want to be with any other?

Keep breathing…but I'd like you to now listen. Be aware of every sound around you. Focus first on your immediate surroundings. What do you hear in this moment? And in this one?

Can you hear anything beyond your immediate surroundings? What do you hear in this moment? Now in this one?

Now, put your hands together — palm-to-palm and fingers-to-fingers. What does that skin-to-skin contact feel like? Focus on only that and be aware of nothing else. Be in this moment with it.

Let every thought and feeling unrelated to this moment dissolve. Keep bringing your focus back to what you are experiencing in this moment, recognizing it as the only true moment.

Your thoughts might strain to move ahead…beyond this moment. Acknowledge each thought, but then refocus on what you hear, on what you smell, on what you're touching. Let everything else go.

And when you feel fully present, or at least *more* present than when you began, open your eyes to this moment and continue with your day.

Exploration • I

On a fresh page in your *Way of the Fool* journal, write the phrase "In this moment, I am…" and complete the sentence or paragraph in a free-flowing, stream-of-consciousness way using the Muse Stream method I described in "Getting Started." Don't think about what to write. Don't censor or second-guess what emerges. Just free onto the page the words, thoughts and feelings that want to emerge and let them reveal to you where you truly are in this moment.

After you have written for a few minutes, begin again using the same phrase: "In this moment, I am…"

Repeat the process at least three more times or until you notice a shift in energy or output. Then take some time to journal on the experience.

Exploration • II

Go for a walk — in nature, around the block, down a busy street or anywhere that offers you some degree of sensory stimulation.

As you walk, do your best to stay in the present moment, focusing only on your five senses and on what you see, hear, touch, smell or taste from breath to breath. As your mind wanders, and it will, acknowledge each stimulus, saying (aloud or silently), "I see/smell/hear/touch/taste the…" and repeat the phrase as you walk, as often as you need to in order to keep focused on the now.

Remember this exercise next time you find yourself pulled out of the present moment by fear or anxiety and let it bring you back — gently and without judgment.

Exploration • III

Each of these suggestions can help quiet your mind and bring you back into the now…

- *Go for a Walk…Anywhere:* It will help clear your head. Incorporate the in-the-moment exercise from Exploration II if that helps.

- *Stretch Yourself:* Take up yoga, tai chi or some other centering discipline that is at the same time physical and meditative.

- *Exercise Your Passion:* When we immerse ourselves in our passion, we often enter into a Zen moment of presence and receptivity. It could be a traditionally creative passion or it could as easily be found in your kitchen, workshop or garden.

- *Meditation:* Listen to a relaxation or guided meditation recording, such as "Listen to Your Heart" in Step #3 or "The Butterfly" meditation in Step #12½. Or use any of this book's meditation scripts, recording it for yourself or having someone else read it to you.

Meditation: The Balloons

Have your Way of the Fool *journal handy to record your thoughts, feelings and impressions, and allow 15 to 20 minutes for this experience.*

Sit down — at your desk, in your favorite chair, in your favorite part of the garden, in your favorite park or on your favorite beach…wherever you feel comfortable, safe and inspired. Or lie down. Do whatever is easiest and most convenient.

Close your eyes, place your hands on your empty lap, or your abdomen if you're lying down, and breathe…in and out slowly, as slowly as you can, for ten breaths.

Breathe more slowly and deeply with each breath and feel yourself relax. Feel each inhalation connect you to your heart, to the moment and to whatever higher power you believe in.

Feel each exhalation flush all fear, doubt and anxiety from your emotional body…flush all worldly concerns from your mind.

As you continue to breathe in and out, let your breath dissolve all tightness from your physical body — from your neck and shoulders, from your chest and abdomen, from your mid- and lower back and from any other place where you cling to stress and tension.

Now, as your breath continues to slow and deepen, focus on your heart and breathe into it and into the only moment that exists: that place of the eternal now.

Now, I would like you to picture yourself in a park or on a beach, holding on to a bunch of brightly colored balloons, each with its own string. There's a slight breeze in the air, and the balloons are bobbing around and bouncing into each other.

As you continue to relax and breathe, you may notice your mind straying from the present moment with a thought about the past or future. Perhaps you are replaying a moment from earlier in your day or from years back. Or perhaps you are thinking ahead — to a bill that needs paying…to an upcoming appointment…or to anything that is not of this moment, that is not of this breath.

Whatever your not-now thought, assign it to one of the balloons. To any balloon. Let a short version of your thought inscribe itself onto the surface of that balloon and, once it has, I would like you to release that balloon. Just let it go and let it float up into the air. Watch it rise higher and higher in the sky, and be aware of it growing smaller and smaller until, finally, it disappears into the distance. As it vanishes from view, let the thought you attached to it vanish as well.

Continue releasing those thought-balloons one-by-one until you are able to stay present in the moment with your breath, then rest in the stillness of the eternal now until you feel complete with the experience.

When you do feel complete, slowly bring your awareness back to your physical body and to your surroundings.

Become conscious of your arms and legs, of your hands and feet, of your neck and shoulders. Move or shake them *gently*. Become aware again of your breath, of your heartbeat.

Notice any ambient sounds — in the room or beyond. What are you hearing? Sensing around you?

Now, become aware of whatever you are sitting or lying on. Let your fingers run over it and feel its texture, its temperature, its solidity, its hardness or softness.

When you're ready, let your eyes open and adjust to the light. Sit up if you're lying down. Connect once again with the physicality and energy of your surroundings.

Finally, and only when you feel it's time, allow yourself to reenter the world, whatever that means to you, from a place of the same moment-to-moment awareness you experienced in the meditation.

In the hours and days ahead, use this thought-balloon imagery to release anything that is pulling you out of the present moment.

Variation: If the balloon image doesn't work for you, or if you simply want to try something different, imagine yourself in a room holding a broom. Each time you find yourself pulled out of the present moment, open the front door and sweep that thought out the door.

My Story: Coda

As I write these words and recall my on-the-road experience of a decade ago, I again find myself in a time of profound financial uncertainty. I would be lying if I claimed not to have had moments of panic in recent weeks over that uncertainty. Yet in revisiting that other time of doubt and worry, I can't help but also revisit the inspiring message of that other time and I can't help but reclaim its priceless gift of presence.

In this moment I have a roof over my head.

In this moment I have a car to get me around.

In this moment I have the resources to pay for food, gas and bills.

In this moment I even have health insurance (which I didn't have a decade ago).

In this moment (as I always have been in every moment) I am wondrously taken care of.

And for all that, I am grateful.

Affirmation

I, *your full name*, live my life moment-to-moment and breath-by-breath, savoring the eternal now. As the Fool that I am, I leave tomorrow's choices, decisions and worries until tomorrow and know that in *this* moment, all is well. And so it is.

Step #3. Follow Your Heart

"An open heart knows no limits."
THE STARQUEST

Imagine you're in a car going for a drive, only you're not the one doing the driving. You're the passenger.

Instead of having to do all the work of steering, navigating, avoiding potholes and looking out for other drivers, you get to watch the scenery unfold around you. You get to sit back and enjoy the ride without having to do any of the planning or any of the driving.

Life can be like that, if you let it. When you put your heart into the driver's seat and let it do the driving, you open yourself to a world of magic and miracles that your conscious mind, as powerful as it is, could never conceive. When you let your heart do the driving, you leave the mundane behind you and speed into the realm of infinite possibility.

Your heart is your intuition. And your intuition is the voice of the Infinite speaking through you. Can you trust that voice?

My Story

In June 1997 I embarked on an odyssey whose consequences I could never have predicted…or imagined. I had been back living in Toronto for only a short while when a voice in my heart urged me to pack all I owned (not a lot) into the back of my Dodge Caravan and head west.

At other times in my life, I would have doubted the message and questioned my sanity.

On that sunny morning, I knew that my only choice was to trust and follow my heart.

For three months I journeyed. I traveled north and west from Toronto along the rugged, forested shores of Lake Huron and Lake Superior, then south and west, crossing Minnesota, North Dakota, South Dakota, Wyoming, Montana, Idaho and Oregon. From the Oregon coast, I slipped south into California, then shot back east, across Nevada and Utah, before dropping into northern Arizona.

Throughout those months, I never planned my next stop. When I tried, my plans were nearly always thwarted by some seemingly outside force. Mostly, I let my heart control the steering wheel and I followed wherever it took me.

It was a magically transformative experience, though not without stress, for it was difficult at times to surrender fully. Part of me longed to plot out an itinerary, to know where I would drive the next week, to know where I would end up. The greater, more courageous part of me trusted in the infinite wisdom of the journey.

Through all the unexpected stops, unanticipated detours and unpredicted forays into uncharted territory, all I could do was trust in each moment and believe that the story I was living would reveal itself — through the living of it.

It did — magnificently.

On the morning of the harvest moon in September, after ninety days of Fool-ish journeying, I drove into Sedona, Arizona. I expected this to be another whistle stop on the road to wherever. Instead, one week grew to two, one month to seven and my life began to transform itself in ways that even a novelist couldn't have plotted.

The Way of the Fool

Only a Fool would step off a cliff and do it not only blindly but joyfully, as the Fool in most tarot decks seems to be doing.

However, the Fool is not blind.

The Fool sees, but not with his eyes. The Fool sees with her heart, and the heart sees all. The heart knows all too, or at least all that is worth knowing.

While the rest of the world trades in the currency of information, banking largely on that which is generated externally in order to weigh its options and forge its decisions, the Fool looks only within. In the Fool's world, there are no options to weigh and no decisions to forge. There is simply the Way of the Fool.

The Way of the Fool is the way of the heart. The Way of the Fool is the way of inner knowingness. The Way of the Fool is the way of intuition and higher guidance. The Way of the Fool is the path of the soul.

The Way of the Fool cannot be found on any chart or map. The Way of the Fool relies on something infinitely more powerful: GPS. Not a traditional, satellite-based global positioning system. A heart-based *God* Positioning System. Wisely, the Fool does not seek out the God of this GPS in any book, building or orthodoxy. The Fool listens for it in his heart.

We all carry a God Positioning System in our hearts, but not all of us choose to hear it when it signals. Of those who happen to hear it, too many choose not to listen. Of those who choose to listen, too many choose not to heed it.

Too many of us choose not to trust.

The Fool hears, listens and heeds. The Fool trusts. So when his God Positioning System directs him to the cliff edge, that is where he goes, with little more than the clothes on his back. And once there, she tunes into the heart frequency of her GPS for her next step — be it off the cliff, back where she came from or in a new direction altogether.

How does that GPS reveal itself to the Fool in us all? Through an intuitive knowingness. Through dreams and visions. Through a gut feeling. Through a twinge, tingle or trembling. Through goosebumps or what Hawaiians call "chicken skin." Through the "meaningful coincidence" of synchronicity.

Where does that infinite wisdom reveal itself? In the peacefulness of a forest glen or in the claxoning cacophony of a bustling city street. On the mirrored surface of a silver lake or through the thundering of a jet engine. In the simple mudras of an ashram meditation or in the complex dissonance of a heavy metal concert.

Our God Positioning System is always and everywhere available and accessible. It waits only to be noticed. The more we notice it, the more frequently it signals. The more we heed it, the more forcefully it signals. The more we trust it, the more flowingly it signals.

When you follow that GPS, you are following your heart. When you follow your heart, you are, in a sense, losing your mind, for you are stepping off the familiar ground of convention and into the unconventional realm of the infinite… of infinite possibility. To borrow from *Harry Potter*, you are stepping onto Platform 9¾ and leaving Muggledom behind as you board the Hogwarts Express, bound for a world of magic beyond anything you could consciously imagine.

When you follow your heart on your version of that train, you travel the Way of the Fool.

A Fool-ish Story

Amelia Earhart dismissed airplanes as "not at all interesting" when she encountered her first at a state fair at age ten. Yet a decade later, when a stunt pilot aimed his plane toward her and a friend, thinking to scare them, a passion she hadn't known she possessed awakened within her. "I did not understand it at the time," she later said, "but I believe that little red airplane said something to me as it swished by."

A few years later, Earhart got her first airplane ride, with famed World War I pilot Frank Hawks, and she was hooked: "By the time I had got two or three hundred feet off the ground, I knew I had to fly."

And she did, breaking record after record after record over the next seventeen years.

Although she disappeared in 1937 during her attempt to fly around the world, Amelia Earhart will always be remembered for her courage, her vision and her groundbreaking achievements…and for following her heart.

"Everyone has oceans to fly, if they have the heart to do it," she is reported to have said. "Is it reckless? Maybe. But what do dreams know of boundaries?"

Your Story

Quick Meditation

Get comfortable, sitting or lying down, and close your eyes. Take a few deep breaths, in and out, guiding your attention away from the rest of your day and into this sacred space of oneness, this sacred time of you-ness.

Place your hand on your heart and feel its rhythm, focusing all your attention on your heartbeat. In this moment, nothing else exists. Only the sound of your heart pumping life throughout your body. Breathe into that sound, into that beat, and think of the sound as an ancient tribal drum sending a message to the next village.

You are the next village. You are where that message is being directed. It's an important message for you. An important message for today. An important message for this moment. What is that message? Listen for it. What does the drumbeat of your heart say? What does it call on you to do? To express? To share? To live? To be?

Listen. Listen for the song of your heart. Listen for its music. Listen for its rhythm and its words. Listen and trust. Listen and follow. Listen and know that the song of your heart will never lead you astray. The song of your heart is the voice of your soul. Welcome it. Honor it. Encourage it. And it will guide you forward.

Take all the time you need to listen to your heart's song. And when you feel complete, thank your heart for its message and thank yourself for having given yourself the gift of this time.

Now, take a few moments to become aware once again

of the rest of your body, feeling your arms and legs, hands and feet…feeling the surface on which you are sitting or lying down. And when you're ready, gently open your eyes and take the song of your heart into the rest of your day.

Ask Yourself These Questions…

Ask yourself these questions in your *Way of the Fool* journal but don't think about the answers. And don't feel you have to answer each question individually if that doesn't feel right.

Let your individual answers (or whatever single answer these questions trigger) emerge freely and honestly, writing them on the Muse Stream in a free-flowing, stream-of-consciousness way where appropriate:

- Where in my life am I censoring or blocking out the voice of my heart?

- Where in my life am I letting it in? In what areas of my life can I let it in more?

- When in my life did I give myself permission to follow my heart, my gut, my intuition, my inner knowingness or my higher guidance? What were the results? (If you feel as though you have never done that, explore why.)

- When in my life have I heard the voice of my heart but not followed it? What were the consequences? How might things have played out differently if I had followed it?

- Where specifically in my life can I be more open to trusting my intuition?

- What can I do in general in my life to foster my

intuition? To nurture and encourage my intuition? To trust my intuition? To act on my intuition? What one step can I take *right now*?

Exploration

As I mentioned here earlier, the voice of your heart is never silent. It is available to you whether you are sitting absolutely still or rocking to your favorite band. At the same time, it can take practice to hear that voice clearly through the busy babel of everyday life. What follows are some of the activities that can create optimal conditions for listening to your heart.

In addition to the activities listed in Exploration III in Step #2, consider these...

- *Meditation:* Do you have a daily meditation practice? Those twenty minutes can help you open to that still, small voice that isn't so small! Just remember that it's not how often you meditate, it's whether you can train yourself to live your life as a meditation.

- *Get out into Nature:* Find a park, nature trail, beach or other quiet spot where you can go for an impromptu amble.

- *Get Moving:* Go for a run or workout.

- *Get Wet:* Soak in the tub or take a long shower.

What other activity (or non-activity) helps you be more receptive? Each time we stop to take a break from our normal doingness, whether in the silence of meditation or in a heart-pumping workout, we open ourselves to the voice of spirit...to the echo of our intuition...to the call of our heart.

Meditation: Listen to Your Heart

Have your Way of the Fool *journal handy to jot down your thoughts, feelings and impressions, and allow at least 30 minutes for this meditative/journaling experience.*

My professionally recorded version is available for download or streaming; it's titled "Write from Your Heart" and is nearly identical to what follows. (Search the relevant site/store for "Mark David Gerson write from your heart.")

See "Getting Started" for details on how to access the recording, as well as for tips on how best to use this book's meditations.

Relax. Close your eyes. Focus on your breath. Breathe deeply. In and out. In and out. In and out. Continue to breathe, in and out, breathing in relaxation, breathing in freedom…allowing any stress, anxiety or tightness to relax into freedom on your breath.

Listen to the rhythm of your heart. Feel it beating. Feel it pumping life throughout your body. Down into your abdomen, groin, legs, feet and toes. Up into your neck and shoulders, your mouth, nose and ears, your eyes. Feel its power in your arms, hands and fingers.

Feel that life force circulate freely, spiraling throughout your body, creating patterns and shapes, colors and sounds. Listen to the rhythm of that life force that is centered in your heart. And in that rhythm, through that rhythm, listen for the voice of your heart.

What does it mean to touch your own heart? Is it physically possible? Can your fingers reach back in on themselves, travel up your arms, past your elbows and shoulders, then down your chest to touch that central mind that, were it truly in charge, would revolutionize your life?

For, yes, your heart is your central mind — a mind more powerful, life-fulfilling and life-affirming than your brain, as powerful and magical a piece of machinery as that is. But that's what it is: a piece of machinery. A wondrous, miraculous machine, but a machine nonetheless.

When we let machines do our living for us, the result is mechanical, soulless and spiritless.

We don't touch others at a deep level when we connect mind-to-mind, though that connection is a powerful and important one. We touch others at a deep level when we connect heart-to-heart.

So, let your fingers reach back in on themselves. See them traveling through your arms…on the inside not the outside.

See them reaching past your wrists and up your forearms, past your elbows and up to your shoulders. Let them stop there for a moment, and from their place deep inside your muscles, bone and tissue, massage and caress the tension from in and around those shoulders.

Feel the release as your fingers press deeply into the soul of your shoulder, releasing all the stress, all the fear, all the tightness, all the anxiety, all the "shoulds."

Notice the word "should." See it write itself out in your mind's eye, and see that this word "should" forms seventy-five percent of the word "shoulder."

It's in our shoulders that we hold all our shoulds. And it's from our shoulders that our shoulds must be released.

Now is the time to massage those shoulds away. Now is the time to un-should-er and feel the lightness return to your shoulders, to your entire body.

Now is the time to let the burden drop from your shoulders. Now is the time to unshoulder all you have been bearing. All the responsibility. All the weight. All the burdens of this time and all time.

Feel your fingers massage them away...out of your shoulders and out of your neck. Let the shoulds dissolve: "I should do this with my life"; "I should live this way"; "I should be careful not to offend"; "I should be careful not to rock the boat"; "I should be what others expect of me"; "I should do what others expect me to do."

Let those shoulds and all shoulds melt under your touch. Let that sense of lightness and freedom you were born with begin to return, even if only for a moment.

Once you feel the return of some of your natural lightness, once you feel some of that un-should-ering, let your fingers continue down to your heart — both the organ at the left side of your chest and the chakra or energy center in the middle of your chest.

Let your fingers continue down, and as they do, let them clear away any cobwebs, let them unlock any doors, gates or walls, let them move in gently and caress that place of love with love.

Let the energy of that love, that aloha, of that place of heart-centeredness, fill your fingertips.

Let the memory of all the love you have experienced, all the loving experiences you have lived, let that memory fill your body so that when, in a few moments, you take it back into your everyday life, it is still infused with that energy, so that this connection to your heart lives on beyond this meditation and can always be reignited.

Continue to breathe, to breathe deeply, as you open your heart and clear away and free all that has been scarred, barricaded and bottled up.

Breathe in the clarity. Breathe in the focus. Breathe in the love, the self-love, the love of your heart, your higher self. Breathe in the aloha.

Continue to breathe, in and out, in and out, for a few more moments. In and out.

In and out.
In and out.
Slowly.
Deeply.
Fully.

As you breathe, listen. Focus your attention on your heart. Focus all your attention on your heart. In this moment, let nothing exist but your heart.

Listen to it. Listen for its voice, for the voice of your soul as expressed through your heart. Listen to your heart. Still yourself and listen.

Your heart has a message for you. A word, a phrase… many words, many phrases. As you continue to focus and listen, you will hear it. Clearly.

Once you begin to hear it, begin to write what you hear, if you feel so called, in your *Way of the Fool* journal.

Continue to listen, paying close attention to all you hear or sense, setting it down in writing if that feels right.

If you hear or sense nothing at this time, don't judge yourself. Simply launch your journaling using this phrase: "My heart speaks to me of…" In either case, write on the Muse Stream, remembering to keep your pen moving across the page, letting it be the medium through which your heart words speak to you.

Write your heart words until you sense completion.

Then hold the silence for a few moments longer, open to anything new your heart has to say.

My Story: Coda

More than twenty years' worth of full moons have risen and set since that September morning when the Way of the Fool guided me to Sedona. Through that time, I have married and divorced and I have become a father and watched my daughter graduate from high school. I have also experienced another open-ended road odyssey — the one I mentioned in Step #2 — and multiplied my literary output, from one unfinished manuscript to more than a dozen published books and three optioned screenplays... an accomplishment I can't quite believe. Also through that time I have called four US states home, in a country that I never imagined would be my home.

This year, the Way of the Fool led me nearly to the Pacific — to Portland. It was neither an expected move nor a conventionally logical one. How could it be when, apart from a few hours eleven years ago, I had never been here. How could it be when, other than a single friend and colleague in the distant suburbs, I knew no one in the area. How could it be when I set out with no savings, no prospects and few possessions. Yet like the Fool I listened to my heart, and when my heart whispered "Portland," I followed.

Unlike the Fool, however, I didn't stand at the cliff edge in unconditional, in-the-moment trust. Unlike the Fool, I arrived with expectations about what my new life in this new place should look like. Unlike the Fool, I worried and fretted when that new life didn't unfold as effortlessly as I thought it should.

It was out of that intense anxiety that *The Way of the Fool* was born. Frankly, I needed to write this book in order to remind *me* of the power and promise of the Fool's journey. I needed it to remind me of the distance I have already traveled along this road. I needed it to remind me of the countless gifts I have received along this road. I needed it to remind me that despite the many bumps, potholes, diversions and bypasses that I have experienced along this road, I have always been supported.

As I write these words, I can't yet know how the Way of the Fool will play out for me in Portland. What I do know is that had I not followed my heart on every stage of this Fool's journey of mine, I would have missed out on so much richness. What I do know is that every time I follow my heart, trusting that the outcome will be more wondrous than anything I could have consciously imagined, it always is. Why would following my heart to Portland be any different?

Affirmation

I, *your full name,* open my mind to the power of my heart and let my intuition guide me along the path of my soul's desire. I walk the Way of the Fool. And so it is.

Step #4. Love Yourself, Love Your Path

"Love yourself. Honor yourself. Celebrate all that you are."
THE BOOK OF MESSAGES:
WRITINGS INSPIRED BY MELCHIZEDEK

It's easy, when you feel as though you have been less than perfect, to beat yourself up. It's easy, when you face setbacks, to doubt your heart, to second-guess your gut, to doubt your intuition.

It's easy, but here's the thing: You *will* make mistakes. It's true. No one is perfect; not even you. That's because the kind of perfection you seek doesn't exist. And those setbacks? Life is going to throw curveballs at you, regularly; that's what life does.

Life isn't a gentle turn on a painted-pony carousel. It's a raucous, daredevil ride on the world's craziest roller coaster.

So embrace your perceived imperfections, respect all aspects of yourself and do your best to enjoy the ride. It's the ride of a lifetime... *your* lifetime!

My Story

IN EARLY NOVEMBER 2004, not long after the polls closed on America's fifty-fifth election, my wife, Aalia, sat me down to tell me that although she still loved me, she felt that she had no choice but to listen to her heart and leave me for a friend of the family. Our marriage of six years was over.

Six more years passed. Aalia and our daughter were still living in Sedona, and I was preparing to move from Albuquerque to Los Angeles. By then Aalia was newly single, and feeling reassured that she could count on the benefit of my same-city support, she decided to follow me back to her hometown with our daughter.

I wonder some days whether I felt called to LA only so that Guinevere could spend her teen years in the city. Certainly, she thrived there. All I know is that two months after I got to California and a month after Aalia and Guinevere followed and moved into their own place, I was gone — following the Way of the Fool back to New Mexico.

I had barely landed back in Albuquerque when Aalia called. Our divorce five years earlier had been amicable. Aalia had wanted no alimony and we'd agreed to keep child support informal and out of the courts. At the time, I had little income and her new partner was supporting her. Now, Aalia was in LA on her own and flailing in fear.

I stood in speechless, guilt-ridden shock in a Costco aisle as she exploded into a rage-filled tirade. "You have to come back to LA," she shouted at me. "You have to get a job. You have to live with us. You have to support us."

I didn't know what to say. Fortunately, I didn't have to say much. In her mounting panic, Aalia left few openings for me to reply. Fifteen minutes later the call dropped.

Shaking with fear, confusion and impotence, I abandoned my shopping cart, fled to the car and began a letter that I wasn't sure I would have the courage to send.

"I've reached a point," I wrote, "where I'm either powerful enough to magnetize to me a life that's worth living or I'm not. I'm not looking for anyone to rescue me. I'm doing what I now know I must do if I'm to continue living. I'll either make it or I won't. I'll either sink or a tidal wave will carry me to shore. I'll either go splat or I'll survive the fall. But I'm no longer prepared to shrink from the full-body, full-hearted attempt."

I acknowledged my responsibility for Guinevere and committed to a modest but regular support. I also insisted that my first responsibility to my daughter was to model the life choices that would enrich her journey in the years ahead. I would not, I wrote, return to LA out of guilt or fear, but only if and when the highest imperative called on me to.

Halfway through the letter, I knew I would have to send it. I knew too that there could be repercussions. I believed that Aalia was emotionally and spiritually evolved enough to recognize the truth of my words. I also recognized how blinding fear could be. Would she turn her back on me? Would she cut off all future contact with our daughter? I knew it was a possibility, however slight. I also knew that the only way to be true to myself was to take the risk.

"I will never stop loving you or Guinevere," I concluded. "But I can only express that love genuinely by loving myself and by honoring what I know in my heart to be true, regardless of fallout or consequences."

Six years almost to the day after my wife left me, I was finally able to love myself and my path enough to leave her.

The Way of the Fool

The Fool is no narcissist. She is not focused on herself to the exclusion of all else. Nor does he need to remind himself of the value and importance of self-love and self-respect. The Fool *is* love. The Fool *is* respect. The Fool embodies the childlike innocence and openness that does not know what it means to question his value or to doubt the value of her journey.

The Fool lives by the true meaning of the fundamental precept of all faiths. To the Fool, "Love thy neighbor as thyself" does not command her to love her neighbor to the exclusion of herself. It calls on him to love his neighbor *as* himself. In other words, the Fool can only love a neighbor *to the extent that she loves herself*. Thus, without an experience of self-love there can be no genuine love for anyone else. For that reason, and in his humanly imperfect way, the Fool treats himself as he would his child or best friend: respectfully and with an unconditional and all-embracing love.

The Fool does not beat herself up for her perceived errors and imperfections. The Fool knows that in their innate imperfection all journeys are perfect, as are all journeyers. Rather, the Fool seeks to acknowledge any errors and imperfections with humility and compassion, endeavoring to recognize their higher purpose and, in so doing, to grow into greater Fool-ishness from them.

The Fool recognizes as well that even were perfection to be possible, it would not be desirable, for its realization would rule out all further growth and strip away all potential for further accomplishment. In perfection, there is nothing left to strive for.

In his wisdom, the Fool is also aware that perfection in nature arrives only at the moment before the onset of decay. The instant after a flower reaches its most glorious and vibrant unfoldment, it begins to die. The instant after a tree achieves the fullness of its verdant luxuriance, its leaves begin to yellow and fall. The Fool knows that perfection represents a sort of death, and he is not ready to die. The Fool chooses life with all its perfectly expressed imperfections

When you embrace the divine perfection of your human imperfection and honor *all* aspects of yourself and of your path, including the painfully uncomfortable ones, you walk the Way of the Fool.

A Fool-ish Story

Broke, with his film career going nowhere (one report has him having been rejected some fifteen hundred times), Sylvester Stallone finally managed to do something that everyone wanted: the screenplay for *Rocky*. In fact, producers wanted it so badly that he was offered more than $300,000 for his script, a monumental amount back in the mid-1970s.

There was one condition, however: Stallone could not play the lead. The studios wanted a big name.

"No deal," Stallone said. Despite his perilous financial situation, he was determined to play Rocky Balboa himself.

In the end, Stallone got his way, but he took a huge pay cut to get it.

Rocky would go on to win three Oscars, including Best Picture. Of its ten nominations, two went to Stallone — for Best Actor and Best Original Screenplay. *Rocky* was also the top-grossing film of 1976, pulling in $225 million worldwide.

Your Story

Quick Meditation

Find a quiet, comfortable place where you can lie down undisturbed for five to ten minutes — longer if you have the time. Close your eyes, rest your arms at your sides and take a few deep breaths, in and out, letting your breath slow with each inhalation and exhalation.

Move your focus to your feet, to your toes…to a single toe, if that's how you need to start. As you breathe in and out, say silently, "I love my toes. I love my path."

Repeat this three times or until you feel a relaxed, tingly sensation in your toes, then move on to other parts of your feet — your soles and arches, for example — then continue up your entire body. To your ankles, calves and shins. To your thighs, your hips, your groin. To your abdomen and chest. To your neck and shoulders. To your arms, hands and fingers. To your jaw, eyes and all the way to the top of your head.

Once you have fully scanned your body, continue by repeating, "I love my body; I love my path." If it feels appropriate to your situation, alternate that mantra with "I respect my body; I respect my path" and/or "I honor my journey; I honor my path."

When you feel complete, rest for a few more minutes in the silence, basking in the love and respect with which you have washed every part of you and in which you have honored your journey and your path.

Then slowly open your eyes and rejoin the world, with that love and respect still vital and alive within you.

Ask Yourself These Questions…

Ask yourself these questions in your *Way of the Fool* journal but don't think about the answers. And don't feel you have to answer each question individually if that doesn't feel right.

Let your individual answers (or whatever single answer these questions trigger) emerge freely and honestly, writing them on the Muse Stream in a free-flowing, stream-of-consciousness way where appropriate:

- Where in my life do I compare myself unfavorably to others? In what ways has that inhibited me or caused me to censor myself? In what other ways has that held me back?

- Where in my life do I see myself as "not enough" or "not good enough"? In what ways has that inhibited me or caused me to censor myself? In what other ways has that held me back?

- Where in my life do I see myself as less than perfect? Physically? Emotionally? Spiritually? Financially? In my job, profession or career? In terms of my relationships with family, friends or colleagues? With my spouse or intimate partner? How do I perceive that imperfection? In what ways do I judge that imperfection? In what ways has that self-judgment played out in my life? In what ways has it held me back?

- In what other ways do I judge and/or criticize myself? In what ways have those negative judgments played out in my life? Held me back?

- In what ways have I beat myself up this week? Today? (Be honest!) How can I make amends? What one act of self-love can I commit to *right now*?

Exploration

One of the most revealing ways we express how we feel about ourselves and our path is also the most unconscious: our language. So often, the words we use are self-critical and disdainful. Too often, we disparage ourselves and denigrate our journey. Nearly always, we have no idea we're doing it.

It's common for us to describe ourselves or our actions as "stupid" or "dumb," to judge an aspect of our journey (or the whole thing) as "pointless" or "futile," to claim that something is "not enough" or "not good enough"… to suggest that we're "not enough" or "not good enough."

In short, we may insist that we love and respect ourselves, but our use of language suggests otherwise.

You don't believe me?

Without censoring yourself, pay attention to your language over the next few days. Listen for the words and phrases that reveal — sometimes subtly, sometimes with alarming clarity — what it is you feel, what it is you fear, what it is you judge. I guarantee that you will be surprised.

For now, here is a selection of words and phrases to watch for and learn from.

- **IMPOSSIBLE.** Any use, unless preceded by the word "not." *You are an innately powerful being of infinite potential. Nothing is impossible.*

- **I'M NOT.** Any use, unless it's to describe something superficial like what you're not wearing or where you're not currently located. *Any "I'm not" negates a part of you. Replace your I'm nots with I ams, and let each "I am" be a declaration of empowerment that braces, bolsters and buttresses your self-esteem, your potential and your journey.*

- **HARD** or **DIFFICULT** or **CHALLENGING.** As in "It's

hard because…" or "It's difficult to…" or "It's challenging to…" *Give no energy to negativity. Whatever it is, just do it.*

- **POINTLESS** or **FUTILE**. Any use. *There is no such thing as a wasted breath, a wasted moment or a wasted experience unless you choose to gain nothing from it. And it is a choice. Each breath, moment and experience is a necessary paving stone on the path that is the Way of the Fool, carrying you forward to the next and to the next one after that.*

- **JUST** or **ONLY**. As in "I'm just a…" or "I've only done…" *Don't belittle your achievements. Celebrate every milestone, regardless of how small it seems to your critical mind.*

- **TRYING**. Any use. *To quote Yoda: "Do or do not. There is no try."*

- **NOT ENOUGH**. Any use. *There is always enough and you are always enough. Period. Don't subscribe to lack in any aspect of your life. Embrace abundance and the abundant, and embrace the abundantly Fool-ish being that you are.*

- **NOT AS GOOD AS.** Any use that puts you or your accomplishments (or anyone else or anyone else's) in a bad light. *Comparisons like these are destructively self-diminishing and pull you out of the moment. Celebrate who you are and where you are. Be the master you are. Be the Fool that you are.*

- **CAN'T** or **DON'T DARE**. Any use. *There is nothing you cannot or dare not do or be. Stop judging and start being.*

- **PROBLEM**. In any context. *There is no problem that*

does not carry within it the seeds of opportunity. Even if the opportunity seems to be invisible in the moment, trust in its existence and shift your focus from the apparent negative to the always-present potential for a redemptive outcome.

- **Supposed To.** In any context. *Where do your "supposed to's" come from? A childhood bully? A teacher? A parent? An older sibling? A partner? A boss? Don't look outside yourself for guidance or validation. Go within. Listen to your heart. Listen to the infinite mind that holds within it the wisdom of the universe and that lives within you, always.*

- **Should.** In any context. *Remember the "Listen to Your Heart" meditation (Step #3) where I invited you to notice that the word "shoulder" begins with the word "should"? Un-should yourself and feel the burdens that you have allowed others to place on your shoulders melt away.*

Try This: Starting today, commit to being more conscious of your words and thoughts. Correct yourself gently and lovingly when those words or thoughts deny your infinite potential, diminish your inner vision or are otherwise critical, judgmental or unsupportive of you or your path. Let your words show you what you think and let them offer you an opportunity to love and respect yourself more.

Meditation: Taming Your Inner Critic

Have your Way of the Fool *journal handy to jot down your thoughts, feelings and impressions, and allow at least 30 minutes for this meditative/journaling experience.*

My professionally recorded version is available for download or streaming; it's nearly identical to what follows. (Search the relevant site/store for "Mark David Gerson inner critic.")

See "Getting Started" for details on how to access the recording and for tips on how best to use this book's meditations.

Sit or lie down in a comfortable position. Close your eyes and take a few deep breaths. Let yourself relax. Feel yourself relax on your breath.

Now, let your shoulders drop…and drop some more. And some more. And some more. Breathe deeply and fully, feeling the breath fill not only your lungs and abdomen but your entire body — from head to toes and back again.

And again. And again.

Feel the breath cleanse you. Feel it dissolve your fears, your anxiety, your stress. Feel it strengthen you, empower you. Feel it protect you, keep you safe. Feel it open your heart. Feel it open your mind.

There have been times in your life when you have been criticized, times in your life when you have been judged. Of course there have. We have all had those experiences. As children. As adolescents. As adults.

Sometimes, the experience rolled off us painlessly. Sometimes, it felt excruciatingly cruel. Sometimes, we forged ahead in spite of it. Sometimes, it shut us down.

It's all normal, all perfect, all part of the human experience. And as with all human experience, we can choose how to react or respond, we can choose how each instance will affect us.

Don't judge how you have reacted or responded in the past. Simply be aware and keep breathing. Fully. Deeply. Allow your breath to once again dissolve any stress or anxiety triggered by unpleasant memories.

Know that you are safe. Protected.

Free from harm of any sort.

From that place of relaxed breathing, from that place of safety, call into your mind, heart and/or consciousness your harshest critic. Perhaps it's someone in your past or present life. A teacher. A parent. A sibling. Another relative. A friend. A school or neighborhood bully. A boss, professional colleague or coworker.

Feel whatever charge you feel around this individual, and breathe. Feel whatever charge you feel around this individual and let that feeling dissolve on your breath.

Now, let that critic transform into some kind of image, something that represents that critic, that stands in for that critic. A symbol. A metaphor. Perhaps it's an animal. Perhaps it's a color or shape. Perhaps it's a snake or serpent. Perhaps it's another human form or another type of form altogether. Or perhaps it doesn't change form at all.

Let it be what it is and know that however it shows up is perfect for you in this moment. Regardless of how it shows up, see it not as an external critic but as an internalized aspect of you, ready to engage with you.

Whatever it is, whoever it is, however it is, greet it and begin a dialogue with it. Have a conversation with it. Engage with it.

Either write this dialogue in your *Way of the Fool* journal as it occurs or let it emerge silently in your heart.

In the first part of your conversation, ask your critic why it judged you so cruelly, what provoked its behavior, what it was afraid of.

If this is an ongoing situation, frame your questions in the present tense.

Listen with an open heart. Respond with an open heart. Allow compassion. Allow understanding. Allow forgiveness. Allow love.

Give yourself thirty seconds of clock time for this part of the experience. Or pause the recording until you are ready to continue.

Be aware that if you are experiencing judgment, there are probably areas in your life where you are expressing judgment. Have compassion for yourself for your judgments. Be understanding. Be forgiving. Be loving. Be open. Be respectful. Toward yourself.

Commit as well to directing those same attitudes toward others, toward anyone you are tempted to criticize harshly.

Now, as you return to the conversation with your critic, ask it how the two of you can work together from this moment forward to bring your work, your path and your life to its fullest, most magnificent potential.

Converse. Discuss. Negotiate. Dialogue. Engage. Silently or in writing.

Again, be loving and compassionate. Be understanding and forgiving. Be respectful. Be open.

Allow another thirty seconds of clock time for this part of the experience. Or, again, pause the recording until you're ready to continue.

Now it's time to bring your encounter to a close. Thank this aspect of yourself for its assistance, for its openness, for its willingness to transform. And commit to this new partnership. Commit too to the spirit of cooperation the two of you have now forged in love and mutual respect.

When you're done, record your experiences and discoveries in your *Way of the Fool* journal. And when you're finished writing and as you move back into your everyday world, remember your commitment to partnership and cooperation.

My Story: Coda

It's sobering to come across the words I wrote Aalia all those years ago and realize that I unwittingly uttered the same ones not too long ago. It has not always been easy for me to love either myself or my path in the face of some of the perceived reversals that I have experienced this year. But if I am to be true to myself and to this path that I was born into and that I have consciously lived for the past three decades, I have no choice but to— I was going to write "try"...until I recalled what I wrote here moments ago and remembered that my words still have at least as much to teach me as yours do you.

As I move forward breath to breath and moment to moment, my only choice is to *be*, to *do* and to *embody* all that I have encouraged you to be, do and embody: the self-love and self-respect that *is* the Way of the Fool.

Affirmation

I, *your full name*, love all aspects of myself, particularly those I view as in any way flawed or imperfect. In each moment and with every breath, I honor myself and my journey as the Fool that I am. And so it is.

Step #5. Be Vulnerable

"Walk the earth naked, clothed only in your truth."
Dialogues with the Divine:
Encounters with My Wisest Self

Share your pain and your passion. Share your dreams and desires. Share your missteps and mistakes. Share your flaws and imperfections. Share your joys. Share your secrets. Share your humanity.

Be vulnerable.

That's what makes you real. That's what makes you interesting. That's what makes you human...what connects you with others...what invites others to connect with you.

Start by opening your heart to yourself. Continue by letting that inner openness, honesty and authenticity move out into the world, infusing every moment of your life. *You* are the light of the world. So shine your light into the world and be the Fool that you are.

My Story

ON THE MORNING OF my forty-second birthday, I packed my few belongings into my Dodge Caravan and for the fifth time in two years, followed my heart along the asphalt road of my soul's journey. My Fool's journey. My destination? A two-room flat in the rural outskirts of Penetanguishene, a summer-resort town a hundred miles north of Toronto on the shores of Lake Huron.

Why was I there? If I needed a reason to satisfy my logical mind, it was to write a new draft of my first novel, *The MoonQuest*. My inner Fool, however, would soon reveal a deeper reason.

My fifth night in my new home, barely asleep for two hours, I awoke from a violent nightmare with the phrase "I just want to say something" echoing in my consciousness. That line, so emblematic of the longstanding blocks to my self-expression that *The MoonQuest* was helping to dissolve, haunted me until I wrote it down. What emerged from those six words was an "inner dialogue" of such transformative depth that I knew I had to keep at it.

I had often turned to inner dialogue to deepen my journaling[1]. But never before had the words cascaded out of me so passionately and, in the ensuing weeks, so frequently.

Although I had not yet heard of Neale Donald Walsch's still-new *Conversations with God*, my writings — which quickly titled themselves *Dialogues with the Divine* — were

---

1. Once in a meditative state, you ask a question then allow the answers to emerge through the "Muse Stream" technique I describe in "Getting Started."

taking on a similar form and tone. Reluctant to expose my uncomfortably raw emotions to the world, I resisted viewing them as part of any sort of manuscript. But the same "Divine" voice that came through on the page so reassuringly had its forceful side. If it didn't immediately demand that I turn these conversations into a book, it did insist that I stop hiding — from myself.

As a frozen Ontario winter began to thaw into spring, I unmasked one demon after another. All found their uncensored way onto the page, ultimately distilled into their single essence: Fear. Fear of sexuality. Fear of judgment. Fear of my vision. Fear of my voice. Fear of my power. Fear of the emptiness from which all creation emerges.

Fear of the unmasking process itself.

My greatest fear, of course, was not about shedding my masks while standing in front of a mirror. It was about removing those masks before stepping out the front door. Self-awareness was terrific. I was all for it. But exposing all those perceived flaws to the world? That left me too vulnerable. That was too dangerous.

"I feel naked," I wrote one day. "I feel exposed. People will laugh. People will judge. People will destroy me, annihilate me. It's too much."

The words that emerged in response were even more terrifying: "Walk the earth naked, clothed only in your truth. Book or no book is not the issue. Coming out is the issue. Being out in the world with your truth is the issue."

This was not about coming out as a gay man. I had done that more than a decade earlier with minimal fallout. It was about coming out as frightened, vulnerable and imperfect. It was about coming out as human.

One evening I printed out three scenes from *The MoonQuest* and took them with me to The Daily Perk, a cafe in nearby Midland. It was Thursday, open-mic night, and I was determined to walk the earth in one of the most naked ways a writer can: by reading from his work-in-progress in front of a live audience.

These were not ordinary scenes. They were scenes of nightmarish horror like none I had ever written, scenes that revealed a dark, violent part of me that I was reluctant to acknowledge, let alone share with a room full of strangers.

These were scenes that made me uncomfortable, that embarrassed me, that made me feel dangerously vulnerable. They were also scenes that I spent the next decade trying to justify excising from the manuscript.

It wasn't until the published book had been out a year that I understood why they were so integral to the story. Actually, I had to be told why — by Michael Hice, who was teaching a class based on the *The MoonQuest* at Unity Santa Fe, which, ironically, nearly banned it from its bookstore because of those controversial scenes.

"*The MoonQuest* is a story about the power of storytelling," Michael explained. "It's a story about what is destroyed when we're prevented from telling our stories and about the healing that occurs when we break through the silence and share those stories with each other."

Put another way, it's about the power of vulnerability.

The Way of the Fool

The Fool of most tarot decks wears no armor or shielding. She carries no dagger, sword or club. The Fool strides forward in joyful innocence, his arms outstretched, eager to embrace the world with neither artifice nor guile.

There is no need to act or pretend when there is nothing to hide. There is no need to shield or insulate when there is nothing to hide. There is no need to appear to be anything other than what he is when there is nothing to hide.

There is no need to hide when the Fool would be hiding only from herself. For at his core he is no different from anyone else.

The Fool has the same defects, faults, flaws and imperfections as every other human on the planet. The only difference is that the Fool does not view those characteristics as defects, faults, flaws or imperfections. She views them as the perfect expression of her humanity…of all humanity.

The Fool carries the same potential for physical pain and emotional torment as every other human on the planet. The only difference is that the Fool does not view those experiences as shameful, dishonorable or inexcusable. He views them as the perfect expression of his humanity…of all humanity.

"If we are all innately the same," the Fool reasons, "what purpose could it possibly serve to conceal those parts of myself that we all are?

"If we are all innately the same, what benefit could there possibly be from me refusing to express that which you also are?

"If we are all innately the same, isn't my tenderness your tenderness? And if my tenderness is your tenderness, how can my open tenderness by anything but a gift — to myself as much as to you?"

The Fool would ask these questions in a reasoning sort of way were the Fool a reasoning sort of being. But the Fool does not need to think through the merits of his vulnerability. The Fool knows, intuitively, instinctively and unquestioningly, that openness is the only path.

There is nothing to hide. There is nothing to hold back. There is only you and me in the unparalleled beauty of our perfectly imperfect humanity. There is only vulnerability. There is only the Way of the Fool.

A Fool-ish Story

Dorothy Allison writes frankly about her working class background and about the poverty and relentless sexual abuse of her childhood.

"Until I started pushing on my own fears, telling the stories that were hardest for me, writing about exactly the things I was most afraid of and unsure about, I wasn't writing worth a damn," she has said.

Sharing her vulnerabilities with the world has earned Allison both praise and censure. A three-time winner of the Lambda Literary Award and a National Book Award finalist, she outraged mainstream feminists with her first book, the poetry collection *The Women Who Hate Me*, and her novel *Bastard Out of Carolina* has been banned nearly as often as it has been lauded.

"I was born in 1949," she told the *Chicago Tribune* in 2012, "and by the time I was ten, I figured out that…I could either be provocative and declamatory, or shy, retiring and scared. And ashamed. I couldn't do much about scared; I was always going to be scared. But I could damn well fight off shame."

Your Story

Quick Meditation

Close your eyes for a moment and take a deep breath. And another. And another. As you relax into your breath, let yourself become aware of one part of yourself that you have been holding back, that you have been hiding… perhaps even from yourself. But certainly from others. Perhaps from one certain other.

Don't dwell on it. Don't work at it. Don't think about it. Let your intuition speak. Let your heart speak. Let your inner Fool speak.

It needn't be big. It needn't be life-altering. But whatever it is, it's significant. It's significant or it would not be showing up for you right now…would not be reminding you of it right now.

What is it? Has it surprised you? Or is it something you have known about, been aware of?

Whatever it is, however big or little it is, can you commit to taking a step toward opening up? Toward being more vulnerable?

Define that step, then make your commitment…your commitment to yourself and your commitment to your humanity.

Ask Yourself These Questions…

Ask yourself these questions in your *Way of the Fool* journal but don't think about the answers. And don't feel you have to answer each question individually if that doesn't feel right.

Let your individual answers (or whatever single answer these questions trigger) emerge freely and honestly, writing them on the Muse Stream in a free-flowing, stream-of-consciousness way where appropriate:

- Where in my life am I refusing to reveal myself to others? To whom? Why?

- Where in my life am I refusing to reveal myself to me? How? Why?

- Where in my life am I holding myself back from experiencing and sharing powerful emotions, especially those emotions I would rather avoid?

- Where in my life am I refusing to be vulnerable and authentic? To be human? What is holding me back?

- Where in my life am I censoring my words or actions for fear of being judged?

- Where in my life am I holding myself back from walking the earth naked, clothed only in my truth?

- In what ways can I begin to share my pain and passion? My dreams and desires? My missteps and mistakes? My imperfection? My joy? In what ways can I begin to come out of hiding? To be less self-conscious? To be more authentic? To be more vulnerable? What one step can I take *right now*? What other steps can I commit to? Tomorrow? The day after that?

Meditation: The Mask

Have your Way of the Fool *journal handy to record your*

thoughts, feelings and impressions. Allow at least 30 minutes for this meditative/journaling experience.

Close your eyes. Let your hands fall to your lap if you're sitting, to your abdomen if you're lying down. Breathe… deeply…in and out…in and out…in and out…letting your breath slow and deepen with each inhalation, with each exhalation.

As you breath in and out, feel your jaw loosen…your shoulders drop…your whole body relax. Feel relaxation course through your body. Feel it carried by your very bloodstream. Feel your bloodstream as a river of calm, relaxation, love and empowerment. Of safety.

Know that at any time during this experience, if anything feels too dangerous to you, all you have to do is take a deep breath and open your eyes. All you have to do is suspend this meditative journey until you feel able to continue. You are safe. You *are* safe.

Continue to breathe, to breathe deeply into this experience…into this journey into the heart of *you*. Focus on your breath, and as you inhale and exhale, I am going to ask you a series of questions. Either answer them in your mind within this meditative experience or pause the meditation while you open your eyes and journal your answers. Whichever works for you. There is no right or wrong way of doing it, just as there is no right or wrong answer to any of these questions.

So…my questions…

What in your life are you self-conscious about? What about yourself do you fear or refuse to experience or express out in the world?

Don't think too hard about this. Simply let a few responses bubble up into your conscious awareness — without judgment and without censorship. Allow yourself to open. Allow yourself to be surprised.

Are you surprised?

Now, go deeper. Look into more places in your life where you are self-conscious. Peer into the dark closets of your reluctance, the dust-filled attics of your concealment, the clammy cellars of your fear.

Where are you embarrassed? Ashamed? Where do you feel inadequate? Where are you afraid of being judged? Where are you holding yourself back? Where are you hiding? Where are you not willing to risk being seen?

Each of those places is a mask you wear out into the world. Perhaps it's a mask you even wear in front of the mirror. But it is a mask. And like all masks, it separates you not only from the rest of the world, but from yourself.

I'd like you focus on one of those masks right now. Just one. Any one. Can you get a sense of what it looks like? You might not experience this visually, and that's okay. There is no right or wrong way to experience any part of this meditation.

Whether or not you can see the mask, what does it feel like? What does it feel like on your face? What does it feel like in your heart? More importantly, perhaps, what is that mask holding you back from feeling? More important still: What is it holding you back from experiencing? From expressing? From being? From becoming?

Journal your answers if that feels right. Or just let them bubble to the surface of your conscious mind. Regardless, sit with them for a few minutes. Let them sit with you.

Do you know why you created that particular mask? Do you have a story that explains it? That justifies it? Of course you do. We all have good and powerful reasons for the masks we wear. Or, more accurately, we *had* good reasons for creating those masks... once upon a time.

But that time is not this time. That time was then, when we needed their protection. This time is now, when we are stronger, braver and more aware than ever that our masks are not ours alone. They are everyone's. And because they are everyone's, they are not only holding us back, they are holding everyone back.

So, whatever your reason for donning that particular mask, however long ago you slipped it on, that reason no longer exists, at least not in the same way it did in that "once upon a time." Can you acknowledge that? And in acknowledging that, can you also acknowledge that that mask is no longer serving you in the ways it was originally designed? And in acknowledging *that*, can you also acknowledge that it is holding you back in some way? Some significant way?

And from that acknowledgment, can you lift that mask from your face? Can you own and accept that it's okay to show your face, to be yourself? To be yourself first *to* yourself. Can you own and accept that it's okay to come out of hiding? To let yourself be seen? To let yourself be vulnerable?

Take a deep breath. As deep as you can. Breathe in all the strength of the universe. Breathe in all the courage of the universe. Breathe in all the love of the universe.

Now, touch your hand to your face. To the mask. And as you do and as you breathe, fully and deeply, let the mask dissolve at your touch. Let it dissolve and reveal the beauty and light that you are. Let it reveal the divine perfection that you are. Let it reveal the humanity that you are.

Be with that unmasked face for a few moments. How does it feel? It's okay to feel scared, if you do. It's natural to feel scared, to feel raw, to feel vulnerable. All that means is that you're feeling human. That's because feeling, whatever it is that you feel, is what it means to be human.

It's also natural to feel lighter, freer, more open to possibility and the fullest expression of your potential.

Feel whatever you feel. Breathe into that feeling. Be okay with that feeling. Sit with that feeling for a few moments. Take some time to let that feeling evolve.

If this is not your first experience with this meditation and you feel able to dissolve another mask, go ahead and do it.

If this is your first experience, be gentle with yourself. Give yourself time to fully integrate and embody what it feels like to have let go this one mask. You can always return tomorrow or next week to remove another.

Regardless, take all the time you now need to remain in this meditative space before becoming once more fully aware of your breath, your physical body and your surroundings as a prelude to stepping back into your everyday life, now lighter, freer and more authentically you.

My Story: Coda

It would take seventeen years for *Dialogues with the Divine*, by then subtitled *Encounters with My Wisest Self*, to "walk the world" as a published book, finally revealing the pain and perceived failings I alone had come to know during my five-month sojourn in Penetanguishene. But the call for me to walk the earth naked, clothed only in my truth would repeat itself again and again in the intervening years — in my writing and in my life.

It repeats itself again in this book, whose 12½ steps I live and relive, not always comfortably, in the writing of them. It repeated it itself the other night when I was on a first date and let myself be more vulnerable with someone I barely knew than I had ever before allowed myself to be in a similar situation. And it will continue to repeat itself as I live and write more and more openly in the days, months and years ahead. For only when I allow myself to be vulnerable, only when I walk the earth naked clothed only in my truth, am I living the Way of the Fool.

Affirmation

I, *your full name*, open my heart to myself and to others and free myself to be my vulnerable, human self in the world. I joyfully walk the earth naked, clothed only in my truth. I joyfully walk the Way of the Fool. And so it is.

Step #6. Let Go

"Your heart will guide you always."
THE MOONQUEST

Imagine a sparrow trying to take off while gripping a rabbit in its claws. Even if it could get off the ground, how high do you think it would go?

Imagine yourself holding onto a large, heavy crate. Even if you were able to stumble forward, how far do you think you would be able to walk?

That rabbit and crate are like the people, places, things, situations, concerns and emotions we cling to because we're afraid we can't live without them, because we clutch at the illusion of security they represent, because we won't trust our heart to lead the way...to keep us safe.

Whatever form they take, such attachments are deadweights that burden us and slow us down, that paralyze and immobilize us, that hold us back and prevent us from soaring into the heights as the beings of unlimited potential that we are.

It's time to unclench. It's time to release.

It's time to let go.

My Story

"Roxy has her destiny; you have yours," I wrote in my journal as part of a *Dialogues with the Divine*-like entry in early 1999. "That those destinies have come together for a time does not mean they are stuck together for all time. Free her to live her destiny. Just as she frees you to live yours."

Roxy was my blonde cocker spaniel. She had entered my life in Toronto in 1994, had traveled with me across half a continent three years later on the journey that carried me into a new life in a new country, and had remained my constant companion — sometimes my sole companion — during my early months in Sedona.

I had now been married for six months and my wife and I were feeling an increasingly powerful call to move to Hawaii. The problem? Roxy. Even if the state's quarantine was less onerous than it had been, all the pet owners I talked to warned me that their dogs were never the same after having gone through it.

I was torn. Intuitively, I knew that a dog as social as Roxy would not do well in that environment and that it would not be humane to subject her to it. That same intuition, however, insisted that Hawaii was the right next move for us.

My journal of the time is filled with tearful pleas for a third option and angry threats, in the absence of a such an alternative, to cancel our move. In the end, after much soul-searching, I knew that I had to let her go so that we could all be free to move forward.

Yet if Roxy wasn't to come with us, what were we to do

with her? We canvassed all our friends; none could take her.

As it turned out, Roxy found her own home.

It was the final Saturday of our final garage sale. As I haggled with bargain-hunters, I noticed a young girl on her knees playing with Roxy. The two were totally involved with each other. When the girl's mother, Leah, shared that she and her husband had been thinking about getting their daughter a dog, I mentioned our Roxy predicament. Leah was intrigued. After we talked more, I offered to bring Roxy to their house the following weekend to see how everyone got along.

The twenty-minute drive to the Weatherbys was emotional, but not nearly as emotional as our arrival would be. When we pulled up to the house and opened the car door, Roxy shot out and raced up the front steps as if it had always been her home. I was startled, relieved and heartbroken.

A few days and many more tears later, I wrote this farewell to Roxy in my journal...

"Goodbye, Roxy. Thank you for all you have given me and done for me. Thank you for all you have shared with me and taught me. Thank you for all the times you have comforted me and made me laugh, all the times you have reminded me of the joy of simplicity and the simplicity of joy. You have taught me well, and I honor and love you for that.

"With both joy and sadness in my heart, I release you. I release you from my future that we may both continue to live in the present. I release you to Savannah and Leah and Don. I release you fully to them, knowing that they will love you as I have, but in their own way, and that you will love them with the fullness you have loved me. I honor you for your journey. I honor you for your love. I honor you for your heart, for your truth and for all that you are. I honor you, love you and release you.

"Goodbye, little one. Goodbye and thank you."

The Way of the Fool

The Fool is dressed for ease of movement. He wears nothing that could restrict or restrain him, carries nothing that could constrict or limit him. The Fool travels light, with room only for the most basic essentials in her tiny bindle. The Fool knows that the greatest distance can be traveled only by those with the most flexibility and the least baggage. So he has let go of all nonessentials. She has even let go of those nonessentials that others might consider essential.

Others might cling to that which offers them the illusion of security, the crutch of comfort. Others might insist that there is no moving forward without the presence of this thing or that person or this emotion…without this care, that concern or this worry. The Fool knows that illusions are little more than delusions and that comfort zones are no better than prisons. The Fool steps past the looking glass of illusion and beyond the confines of comfort to launch his journey, shedding all encumbrances.

Like the snake that casts off its old skin with each new season, the Fool allows that which no longer serves her to fall away in an organic process that requires neither thought nor analysis. Rather, the practice is intuitive, instinctive and comes from the heart. It simply is.

The Way of the Fool is the path of letting go. The Way of the Fool is the path of highest good. The Way of the Fool is the path of trust. The Way of the Fool is the path of the heart.

A Fool-ish Story

There's a coronation scene in *The MoonQuest* where King Fortas, having abdicated in favor of his son, Kyri, passes his crown, scepter and royal robes and regalia to the young man. Kyri has no sooner donned all the symbols of his father's kingship when the oracle presiding over the ceremony announces that the prince must "let go all that encumbers him to the old reign."

As Kyri strips and each symbol of his father's monarchy is then consigned to a burning pyre, the crowd chants, "The past is passed, we let it go."

Yet Kyri finds that he can't fully let the past go…can't fully let his father go…can't fully step into the new power that is his to claim. "You are not my subject," he says to the old man. "You are ever my lord."

Hearing this, the crowd grows restless, and its increasingly vocal chants calling for Fortas's reinstatement threaten the new reign before it has even begun.

"The past is not your lord," Fortas counsels Kyri. "Set your sights on the future, my son, my king. Set your sights on the future by seeing to the present. Don't let your vision linger longingly on the past. Let it go, my son. Let it all go."

Like Kyri, we disempower ourselves by clinging to any vestige of a past that no longer serves us. The past *is* passed, and by letting it go we, too, claim our sovereignty.

Let it go. Let it all go.

Your Story

Meditation: Letting Go

Have your Way of the Fool *journal handy to record your thoughts, feelings and impressions. Allow at least 40 minutes for this meditative/journaling experience.*

Find a quiet spot where you can sit or lie down undisturbed for the next 30 to 45 minutes. Then get comfortable, close your eyes and relax.

Take a few deep breaths in and out…in and out…in and out…letting your breath dissolve all the stresses and strains of your day. Letting your breath relax your body and your mind and your spirit. Letting your breath connect you powerfully with your deepest guidance and intuition. With your heart.

As you continue to inhale and exhale slowly and fully, scan your body for any knots of tension. Wherever you find them, let your breath untangle and dissolve them.

Now, scan your life as it is now for anything in it that is superfluous. "Superfluous" does not have to mean a bad or harmful thing. It might be something you don't need anymore…something you have outgrown…something that's holding you back in some way.

It could be a person, a place, an object, an emotion, a situation, a worry or a concern. It could be some way you view or describe yourself. It could be any of those, some combination of those or something else altogether. It could be something heavy and serious, or it could be something much lighter.

And there could be more than one thing or person that falls into this category.

Don't scan with your logical mind. Scan with your heart. Scan with that part of you that knows all, that sees all, that fears nothing. Scan with that part of you that is connected directly with the infinite wisdom of the universe, with your unlimited potential and with your highest path and highest good.

Now, remove your direct focus from your breath and let your breathing return to normal, even as you continue to go deep within in order to answer this next series of questions.

As I ask each of these questions, you might want to open your eyes just long enough to reach for your *Way of the Fool* journal and jot down your first thoughts. Always go with first thoughts. Hesitation is your doubting, censoring mind at work. Your fearful mind. Second thoughts are also produced by your doubting, censoring mind. So let whatever first bubbles up into your conscious mind be the answer you accept, the answer you trust, the answer you go with. The answer you act on when it is time act.

Okay, here are the questions I'd like you to ask yourself. First...

- What one thing in my life do I no longer need, today? Right now? In this moment?

As I mentioned earlier, it can be a person, an object, an emotion, a situation, an attitude, a worry or a concern. It can be a way you view or describe yourself. It can be any of those, some combination of those or something else altogether.

It can be something critical or serious, or it can be something not quite so monumental but still significant. As long it is significant to you in whatever way it is, that's all that matters.

Don't think about it. Don't second-guess it. Don't judge it. It doesn't even have to make logical or conventional sense. Nor do you have to act on it in any way in this moment. You are simply asking the question.

There are no right or wrong answers to this question or to any of these questions. Wherever your awareness first lands is the perfect answer for today. For this moment. For right now. Remember to always go with first thoughts, whatever they are.

So what is it? Who is it? It doesn't matter how overwhelming your answer might be, or how frightening, or even how strange. Just go with it. Be with it.

Now, take a moment to jot it down. Don't analyze it. Just note it.

Pause the recording if you need to, then restart it when you are ready.

Here's another question…

Think back to your previous answer. Whatever it is, whoever it is, ask yourself this:

- How long has this person, object, emotion, situation, attitude, worry or concern been unnecessary to my life?

- How long has it been getting in my way, however it is getting in my way? Can I pinpoint the moment? It could be right now. It could have become unnecessary months or years ago.

Perhaps "unnecessary" is the wrong word for whatever it is. Perhaps it's getting in your way in some minor or major way. If it's a person or a relationship, perhaps you're holding each other back in some minor or major way. Once again, the scale or scope is not important. What's important is the awareness…the recognition.

Note that I am not asking how long this "whatever it

is" has been in your life. I am asking how long it has been *unnecessary* to your life. Or superfluous. Or in the way in some meaningful way.

It very well may have served an important and valuable purpose once upon a time. At some point, though, it moved into this new category, rendering it problematic in some way.

Now, take a moment to record your answer to that question. Again, how long has this person, object, emotion, situation, attitude, worry or concern — or whatever it is — been unnecessary in whatever way it has been unnecessary?

Pause the recording if you need to; restart it when you are ready.

Another question...

Whatever it is you have identified, whoever it is you have identified, ask yourself this:

- How did I find myself holding on to it? Clinging to it? What was the trigger?

- If it was originally necessary or helpful, in what way was it necessary or helpful? What did it protect me from? How did it make my life easier?

- Whenever it entered my life to serve some valuable purpose, that value didn't last. Something changed. Suddenly or gradually. What was it? What was it that changed things for me?

If there is no clinging involved, if you have just had the instant realization that it's time to let something or someone go *before* a problem emerges, that's okay. Note that.

Again, pause the recording to jot down whatever notes you need to. Restart the recording when you're finished.

One final question, perhaps the most important question of all:

- Whatever it is, whoever it is, how can I let it go? How can I release it? Or if it doesn't need to be entirely released at this time, how can I transform it from something that is somehow in my way to something that is helpful?
- What first steps can I take today to let it go? What one step can I take now, as soon as I have finished this meditation?

You don't have to know or have all the steps in this moment. If you have more than one, that's awesome. For now, for today, for this moment, all you need is a first step. All you need is a way to begin.

Pause the recording one final time to jot that down. And when you're ready to continue, restart it.

Before you bring yourself out of this meditative space to rejoin your everyday world, open your journal again and, taking the notes you have made to this point, record your feelings about this process, about what it has called on you to do. Record your fears and hesitations and doubts. But also record how you will feel once you have let this go from your life or transformed it in some substantive way…once you have removed or dissolved this barrier, this burden, this hindrance, this weight.

If other steps come to you as part of this letting go, jot them down as well.

Take all the time you need for this final step, and when you are finished, commit in writing to continuing and completing this process. And commit to a reasonable and practical timetable.

Finally, as we all have more than one something or someone in our life that is somehow preventing us from moving forward in some meaningful way, a someone or something that it would be helpful for us to let go of or transform our relationship with, repeat this meditation and process as often as you need to in order to continue lightening your load on the Way of the Fool.

Exploration

Life is an act of pilgrimage. We set out on a journey, often intent on a particular direction and destination. Yet if we are true to our heart, we free it to carry us where it will. The resulting journey is a pilgrimage…a voyage of discovery and self-discovery along the Way of the Fool.

How has your life and journey been a pilgrimage? What has that pilgrimage revealed to you? About yourself? About your passion and purpose? About your life? About the world? Explore your answers to these questions in your *Way of the Fool* journal, not analytically but heartfully, without self-censorship or second-guessing.

My Story: Coda

On December 14, 2004, I got ready to say goodbye to my five-year-old daughter, not knowing when I would see her again. My marriage had ended six weeks earlier and all my inner guidance was urging me to leave town, even if it meant leaving Guinevere behind.

I parked outside the restaurant where she and her mother were having brunch, sat in the car for a few shaky minutes, then called my wife on my cell. She brought Guinevere out to me and left us alone.

I must have told my daughter that I loved her, that I would love her always and forever, wherever I was, and that I would see her soon. I must have reminded her that she could hear me on the CD I had recorded for her of all the bedtime songs I had sung to her nightly since she was born. I must have said all that, but I remember nothing. All I remember is watching her disappear back into the restaurant and driving away, sobbing.

Until that moment, releasing Roxy had been my most heartbreaking letting-go. This was worse. Much worse. The Way of the Fool is rarely a comfortable one.

Affirmation

I, *your full name*, release and let go all that no longer serves me on my journey, trusting my heart to guide me forward to my highest good. I embrace the Fool that I am. And so it is.

Step #7. Take Risks

"'You must go,' the wind insists.
"'Go where?' Kyri asks. 'There is nowhere to go.
I will die out there.'
"'Stay, and you are already dead,'
the wind replies."
THE MOONQUEST

We enter into this lifetime in the leap of faith that our soul takes into the being in our mother's womb. We take that one huge leap only to discover that such leaps never cease being demanded of us.

First one leap into the unknown, then another, then another, then another, until that instant when with our final breath, we take the ultimate leap of faith...into the unknowable.

Each leap represents a greater risk. Each leap challenges us more profoundly. Yet each leap on the path to that ultimate one opens us to greater miracles and richer rewards.

And with each of those leaps, we feel more alive, more in the flow and more aligned with our heart's desire and our soul's passion.

Always.

Are you ready to take your next leap of faith? Are you ready to trust, let go and leap? Are you ready to risk all for your heart's desire?

"What if I fail?" I hear you ask.

What if you don't?

My Story

WHEN I RETURNED TO Albuquerque from speaking at the Conscious Life Expo in Los Angeles in early 2010, I knew that it was time for me to make the move to Southern California that I had been contemplating for several years. Over the next months I made several exploratory visits to LA and each time I returned more certain of the rightness of this next step.

The only problem was that the surer I felt about Los Angeles, the more my Albuquerque life shut down. Book sales dried up. Coaching clients wrapped up their work with me and no new ones materialized to take their place. In fact, no money at all was coming in, not even to meet the most trifling expenses. How would I continue to survive in New Mexico, let alone finance a move to California?

I felt paralyzed, impotent, angry and scared. Mostly scared. Like *The MoonQuest*'s Kyri in the quote that opens Step #7, my desert sanctuary had ceased to function for me. I knew I needed to leave. Yet I couldn't see how.

"Give notice on your condo," my friend Sander insisted in his tough-love way when he called from Toronto one morning in the midst of my self-pitying despair. "You have to do it."

I knew he was right. Yet it was a leap of faith I couldn't see taking. How could I give up my home when there was no money to move and no money to land? There wasn't even money to pay my current bills.

Even as I argued and resisted, I knew my resistance was

futile. I knew in my heart that the only way to live was to leave. I knew too that the only way to leave would be to take a leap of faith off the highest cliff I had ever encountered and to trust that, as I always had been, I would be supported.

I wish I could report that I surrendered joyfully and gracefully. I didn't. I was childish, churlish, petulant and argumentative…more paralyzed by fear than I had been in decades. Yet deep down, I knew I had no choice: I would have to give notice on my rental and step trustingly into the void — as I had done so often in the past, just as the Fool does.

My miracle showed up within the hour, even before I had a chance to write and mail my letter of notice to the property manager. It came in the form of a phone call from someone I barely knew.

Adam and I had met online months earlier and had talked only a handful of times since. "I was driving to the gym," he said, "and I knew I had to call you. I don't know why."

I didn't either. We chatted amiably for an hour and, toward the end of our conversation, I mentioned that I was preparing to move to LA — on faith, with no sense of how I would either get there or live there.

"I've got plenty of space," Adam surprised himself by saying. "Stay with me." His street name? Spirit.

The Way of the Fool

The Fool does not view herself as a risk-taker. A risk-taker weighs the odds before he acts, before he "takes a chance." The Fool, however, neither acknowledges nor recognizes "odds." If she were to do so, she would be curtailing her innately unlimited potential and placing her fate in the hands of a bookmaker's all-too finite calculations. He would be trading the miracle of infinite possibility for the inherent limitation of conventional probability.

Nor does the Fool need to strain to let go of anything, for there is nothing and no one that the Fool clings to (Step #6). Living moment-to-moment as she does, the Fool values all that is present in each breath but carries nothing into the next. Each inhalation is a new birth into a new life; each exhalation, a death.

Like every newborn, the Fool begins each moment with nothing. He ends each moment the same way. There is a reason her numerical representation in the tarot deck is 0.

The Fool may not view himself as a risk-taker, but from our perspective he is the ultimate daredevil, journeying where no one but the foolish would dare go, each step a greater leap into danger than the last.

Yet danger only exists in a mind that refuses faith. Not faith in some theoretical deity, but faith of the heart. We too would leave fear behind if we trusted our intuition to speak with the voice of our highest imperative and if our leaps were truly made in faith.

In the perfection of our imperfect humanity, fearlessness may not be an option. Fortunately, courage is all we need to walk the Way of the Fool. Courage acknowledges the presence of fear but acts in spite of it. Courage walks into the fear and through it to the other side. Courage is the willingness to ignore the risk and take that leap of faith.

A Fool-ish Story

Although born into a wealthy Baltimore family, Virginia Hall had little interest in settling into the privileged marriage that was expected of women of her class in the 1920s and 1930s. Virginia Hall was a risk-taker who yearned for adventure.

She got more than she bargained for. While hunting in Turkey, Hall accidentally shot herself in the leg. Gangrene set in, her left leg was amputated below the knee and she learned to get around with a wooden leg that she named "Cuthbert."

In France when World War II broke out, Hall volunteered to drive an ambulance for the French, fleeing to England when the Nazis invaded. It was there that a chance encounter put her in contact with British intelligence.

That's when the real risk-filled adventure kicked in for Virginia Hall: This one-legged American became one of the first British spies sent into Nazi-occupied France in 1941. There, she became one of the most effective undercover operatives of the war, so much so that the Gestapo dubbed her "the most dangerous of all Allied spies."

When British intelligence considered it too risky to send her back into France, Hall signed up with the US Office of Strategic Services, precursor to the CIA. In one OSS report, Hall's team was credited with having derailed freight trains, blown up bridges, killed more than a hundred Nazis and captured five hundred more.

After the war, Hall was awarded the Distinguished Service Cross, one of the highest US military honors for bravery in combat, the only woman to receive the award for service during World War II.

Only a Fool would take the risks Virginia Hall did. Those risks helped change the course of a war…and of history.

Your Story

Ask Yourself These Questions…

Ask yourself these questions in your *Way of the Fool* journal but don't think about the answers. And don't feel you have to answer each question individually if that doesn't feel right.

Let your individual answers (or whatever single answer these questions trigger) emerge freely and honestly, writing them on the Muse Stream in a free-flowing, stream-of-consciousness way where appropriate.

Before you reflect on the following questions, though, be aware that risk is highly subjective. What feels risky to me might not feel at all risky to you, and vice versa.

In exploring risk in your life, recognize that it's not the objective scale or importance of an action that determines its riskiness. It's how it feels to you. Don't judge those risks…and don't judge yourself!

I. "You've got to go out on a limb," humorist Will Rogers is reputed to have said, "because that's where the fruit is."

- Where am I going out on a limb and taking risks in my life? Not random risks, but risks that speak to my passion, that answer the call of some deep inner imperative, that follow the voice of my heart.

- Where am I avoiding risk? Where am I staying on the ground and clinging to the perceived safety of the tree trunk?

- Where am I taking a leap of faith into the unknown? Where am I stuck in convention, playing it safe?

- Where can I acknowledge my fear, but not let it paralyze me? Where can I take a risk?
- What one courageous step can I take today, *now*, to commit to going out on a limb?

II. We have all experienced moments when fear has paralyzed us and prevented us from acting…when we have walked away from something because it felt as though the risk was too great.

Has that happened to you? Can you think of a situation in your life when you walked away from something — perhaps something you desired deeply — because it felt as though the risk was too great?

This is not a moment for looking back in regret. Rather, it's an opportunity to reflect on that "road not taken" from today's place of greater wisdom and courage.

- What did I learn from that experience?
- How can I apply what I learned to a current life choice?
- What risk can I now take as a result?

III. Not all leaps of faith land us where we expect. Nor do all risks play out as anticipated. Yet wherever the Way of the Fool carries us, even if it is far from our planned destination, gifts always await us.

- What risks have you taken in your life where the result could be described as conventionally successful? Revisit that experience and feel again the inner strength and courage that allowed you to take that risk. Revisit that experience and again feel the clear and evident gifts and rewards.

- What risks have you taken in your life where

the result wasn't what you expected? Where you felt, perhaps, as though you failed? Or where for whatever reason you regretted having taken that leap? Pick one of those regrets or perceived failures and find the gift in that experience. It's there; I promise you!

Quick Meditation

As I have invited you to do before, close your eyes for a minute, take a deep breath, and connect with one risk, even a tiny one, that you're prepared to take in order to live a fuller, more authentic life…one that's true to your heart, your soul and your passion. Connect with that risk and know that, in faith, nothing is truly a risk. Connect with it and commit to taking it. Now.

My Story: Coda

Ten weeks after I moved into Adam's, I was on the road again…on my way back to Albuquerque. On the surface it looked as though my leap of faith had been a disaster, as though my risk had not been worth taking. What had I accomplished, other than further wrecking my finances and leaving me potentially homeless?

A lot, as it turned out. As brief as it was, my time at Adam's had transformed a casual acquaintance into a treasured friend. And the leap of faith I took by leaving not only turned another acquaintance into a close friend but launched the most creatively productive period of my life…at least to that point.

There is no experience in life that does not carry within it the seeds of opportunity and the potential for a redemptive outcome. I remind myself of that daily here in Portland, where new leaps of faith continue to be demanded of me and where, like the Fool, I leap into void after void after void.

The Way of the Fool is the way of surrender. The Way of the Fool is the way of faith.

Affirmation

I, *your full name*, trust fully, surrender completely and risk all as I open to the voice of my heart and let it guide me along the Way of the Fool. And so it is.

Step #8. Live Your Passion

"It is passion that has kept me alive and healthy. Passion for causes. Passion for love. Passion for life."
THE EMMELINE PAPERS

Find your passion and embrace it. Passionately. Then commit to that passion, unconditionally.

It doesn't have to be some grand passion. It could be a passion for your garden or your passion for travel. It could be your passion for life, for your path...your passion for the journey.

Whatever it is and however you define it, be it. Leap into it with every cell. Immerse yourself into it with every drop of blood that flows through your veins.

Let your passion inform every choice, every decision, every step, every word. And live the Way of Fool.

My Story

THE FIRST TIME MY writing mentor invited me to teach the course she'd created, a course that had revolutionized my creative and spiritual life when I took it, I declined. The second time she asked, I also said no. When she approached me a third time, I didn't dare turn her down on the spot. Instead, I asked for time to think about it.

That night I had a dream. It was a dream I couldn't ignore.

I had only recently begun paying close attention to my dreams — recording them, journaling about them and doing my best to heed any messages they seemed to be communicating. As with most dreams, however, mine were often too convoluted and surreal to easily interpret.

This wasn't one of them.

The time: World War I. The players: Beth and her overprotective husband, George. The situation: Beth is seriously injured when the jeep they're driving hits a land mine. Now, George sits by Beth's hospital bed, doing his best to discourage her from teaching, a pursuit he considers life-threateningly dangerous.

"I must teach," Beth proclaims in a tone that brooks no argument.

As the dream fades on her words, I hear the Hebrew prayer that is sung every Saturday morning in synagogue when the Torah scroll — the law of God — is held up for the congregation to see before it is returned to the ark: *V'zot ha-torah asher sam Moshe lifnei b'nai Yisrael, al pi*

Adonai b'yad Moshe. "This is the law that Moses placed before the children of Israel: from the mouth of God to the hand of Moses."

I didn't know what it would mean to say yes to my mentor. I knew only that even if the protective "George" aspect of me was frightened for my safety, I had no choice. As the "Beth" part of me declared with such force and passion: I had to teach.

A few months later, guided by my mentor, I taught my first writing course — the one she had created. It wasn't long, though, before I was developing my own material and facilitating my own workshops, embracing a passion I hadn't realized I'd had.

That was more than thirty years ago, and my passion for inspiring others to embrace their passion hasn't dimmed. I have been teaching, mentoring and coaching new and seasoned writers ever since.

Now, with the new material in this book, I am unexpectedly expanding my work and my passion to more fully include non-writers. The Way of the Fool is full of surprises.

The Way of the Fool

In the life of the Fool, passion is all there is. There is no moment when she is uncommitted, unenthusiastic or half-hearted. There is no moment when he is detached, disengaged or disconnected. She leaves no opening in her day to be unoriginal, uninspired or unimaginative. He leaves no opening in his to be disheartened, discouraged or dispirited. The Fool embraces each day with delight... leaps into each instant with wholehearted fervor...dives into every encounter with gusto.

The Way of the Fool is not a part-time path. The Fool does not relegate her passion to nights and weekends or disjointed fragments of "free time." Each breath is breathed with passion. Each step is taken with passion. Each word is spoken with passion. Each thought is steeped in passion. Each action is informed by passion. There is no moment, waking or sleeping, during which passion is not his compass, does not light her way.

When you live your passion and free your passion to live through you, you walk the Way of the Fool.

A Fool-ish Story

When Connie Willis quit her teaching job to raise her daughter, she decided that it was time to start writing professionally, because that was something she could do at home.

What Willis discovered was something radically different. "I never had, for the next eighteen years, more than fifteen minutes at my disposal," the science fiction author would later reveal in a TVOntario interview, "and I learned that if I really wanted to be a writer, I couldn't wait until I had more than fifteen minutes at my disposal."

Willis learned to write in whatever odds and ends of time showed up for her: in the orthodontist's waiting room, at football and basketball games, in the car outside her daughter's school, at her husband's gymnastic classes.

"You've got to write today," she continued, "when you have the time that you have."

Whatever your passion, however it shows up in your life, the same is true for you. There is always time. Seek it out.

Your Story

Exploration • I

Too often we labor under the false assumption that our lives are too busy to accommodate the things we're most passionate about. "I'll wait until the kids grow up and are out of the house," we say. Or, "I'll do it when I retire." Why wait until more than half your life is over to start living it?

Let's look at how you currently spend your time and at where you are sacrificing your passion for activities that fill time but don't speak to your heart's desire.

For each of the following items, estimate (honestly!) both a daily and a weekly average in your *Way of the Fool* journal. Why both? Because in most of our lives, not all days are created equal. (Don't worry: I'm not going to ask you to give up any of these activities.)

How much time each day/week do you spend...

1. Watching TV?
2. Watching Netflix or other streaming services?
3. Reading magazines (online or in print)?
4. Reading newspapers or following online news?
5. On Facebook and other social media?
6. Watching YouTube or other videos?
7. Playing video or other online games?
8. On other distracting activities on any electronic device?

9. On dinner and/or drinks with friends?

10. Going to clubs, sporting events, movies?

11. On other pursuits and activities, online or off, that you can honestly categorize as needless, superfluous, distracting, time-wasting or otherwise non-critical?

12. Commuting (not in a car you're driving)?

Take your totals and divide them by half. Can you free up that daily or weekly time to devote to something you're passionate about? To something that makes you feel alive? To something that makes life worth living? What about if you divide it by a third? By a quarter?

(Note that when it comes to #12, commuting time, there is nothing you have to stop doing. You simply have to find a way to devote some of that travel time to your passion.)

Exploration • II

What kinds of distractions do you typically succumb to? For a week, inventory all the distractions that keep you from accessing, experiencing and expressing your passion.

Don't judge yourself or be hypercritical. Just notice all the energy you have put into not acting on your heart's desire.

As each day passes notice if your heightened awareness has moved you to give up some of those distractions in favor of more "passion time."

Meditation: Embrace Your Dreams

Have your Way of the Fool *journal handy to record your*

thoughts, feelings and impressions. Allow at least 15 minutes for this meditative/journaling experience.

Settle into a quiet, comfortable place where you won't be disturbed for fifteen or twenty minutes. Close your eyes, relax and focus on your breath — breathing in and out, in and out, in and out...slowly, deeply...then more slowly, more deeply.

Let your breath dissolve all the cares and worries of your day, all the distractions that keep you from focusing on your most heartfelt dreams. Breathe into your heart, that central brain that knows all and fears nothing, that is the source of all, that is the dwelling place of all your deepest desires...your soul's desire and imperative...your hopes, dreams and passions.

Without thinking, just letting whatever first bubbles up into your awareness, answer the following question. Remember to not second-guess yourself or censor yourself, and remember to go with first thoughts. Always first thoughts.

What is my biggest, deepest dream for myself?

Remember: No thinking, no analyzing. Whatever comes up first, whether or not it seems to make conventional sense or seems possible to realize.

Again: What is my biggest, deepest dream for myself?

Take a moment to journal your answer, then continue on.

Were you surprised by what came up? Was it something you have long suspected? Was it something you have always known? Or was it something that, until this moment, you had no conscious awareness of?

Whatever your deepest dream, whatever your most profound passion, know that however improbable it may seem in this moment, it is not impossible. Nearly every success story begins with an "impossible" dream. Nearly every "overnight success" was years in the making.

Too often, we are so convinced that our dreams are unattainable that we stuff them into the back of a drawer — so far back that we forget about them. So, what about yours? Have you abandoned them?

Picture that drawer, that repository of your abandoned dreams. Picture it and now open it. Reach your hand in. Gently. Whatever that dream is, touch it. Reconnect with it. Reconnect with yourself.

Now is the time to put your dream into action. It doesn't matter whether you can give it five minutes a day or five hours. It doesn't matter whether you see it as improbable or even impossible.

Every journey starts with a single step. What one step can you take today, right now, toward making your dream a reality…to begin to *real*-ize it? Whatever it is, note it in your *Way of the Fool* journal. Then write on the Muse Stream from the phrase "I am ready to live my dream…" If you know now what your dreams are, let this be a statement of commitment and part of your first step toward realizing them. If you don't, let yourself discover dreams you never knew you had through this exploration.

Open your heart to your dreams. Open your heart to your vision. Open your heart to yourself. Open your heart to your life. Say yes to you!

Exploration • III

Embracing your passion full-time doesn't have to mean giving up your day job. It means that however you spend your days, you endeavor to live each moment with passion. It means that you free your passion to express through you regardless of what you're doing and where you're doing it. At the same time, it's a call to seek out what excites you, animates you and fires you up and to be open to all the ways that your passion can became a greater and greater part of your life…and your living.

Ask Yourself These Questions…

Ask yourself these questions in your *Way of the Fool* journal but don't think about the answers. And don't feel you have to answer each question individually if that doesn't feel right.

Let your individual answers (or whatever single answer these questions trigger) emerge freely and honestly, writing them on the Muse Stream in a free-flowing, stream-of-consciousness way where appropriate.

I. Identifying what brings us joy and what makes us feel most alive is a first step toward inviting more passion into our lives.

- Where and when is passion present in my life? How does it feel in those moments when I am able to access, experience and express that passion?

- Where and when is passion absent from my life? How does that feel? What can I do to inject more passion into those moments, to live those moments more fully, regardless of what I'm doing?

- What excites me, animates me and fires me up? What more than anything else would I (or do I already) find joy in doing? How do I feel when I'm involved in it? When I'm away from it? How can I create more opportunities in my life to feel and experience that kind of passion?

- Is there an activity in my life that when I am

engaged in it, I lose all awareness of time? What is it? What other sensations or emotions does that activity spark within me? How can I devote more time and energy to that activity or to a similar one?

- Can I think of a time in my life when I felt most alive, most vibrant, most vigorous? What was I doing? What else was I feeling? What can I do in my life to recreate that feeling? What one step can I commit to *right now*?

II. "Act as though and make it so," I wrote in my *Acts of Surrender* memoir, and it's a statement that I still do my best to apply to my life. When we act as though the life we desire — our passion, if you will — is already in place, our action becomes part of the magic that makes it possible.

- If money were no object, how would I be spending my time? My life? How would I be experiencing and expressing my passion?

- What one step can I commit to *right now* toward bringing my passion and my money-is-no-object desire — or more of it — into my life?

My Story: Coda

If my passion for teaching startled me, perhaps it shouldn't have. My passion for writing had already taken me by surprise.

I like to joke that my Muse tricked me into writing. Through public school and most of university, I did everything I could to avoid writing. But my Muse had other plans, and I was slowly and subtly transformed into the writer I never thought I wanted to be.

For example, during my final two years of high school, I was persuaded to do publicity for a pair of student musicals — a task that involved writing. As if that weren't enough, I continued to do theater publicity (and related writing) through college. Not surprisingly, my first two jobs out of university were in public relations. More writing.

By my late-twenties I was a writing (and editing) full-time as a freelancer — for newspapers and magazines, as well as for corporate, government and institutional clients. Yet it would take another dozen years before I was able to move from a teller of others' tales to a teller of my own, a transition that occurred as a direct result of the writing course I would later find myself teaching.

Sometimes, we are gifted early in life with a clear sense of our passion. Sometimes, it reveals itself later and more gradually. Regardless, when we acknowledge, experience and express our passion — when we *live* it — we are walking the Way of the Fool.

Affirmation

I, *your full name*, surrender to my soul's desire that I might experience and express it more fully in my life. I free those passions that I am aware of to deepen within me and those that lie hidden to reveal themselves to me. I walk the Way of the Fool. And so it is.

Step #9. Don't Give Up

"It's never too late to follow your dreams."
SARA'S YEAR

In my novel *Sara's Year*, two of the characters enter their teen years with powerful dreams and ambitions. One yearns to be a writer; the other, an artist.

By the time they reach their early twenties, however, both dreams have been abandoned. Life has a way of getting in the way, when we let it...and both those women did.

The good news for one of the two is that, ultimately, she not only revives a dream that she believed to have been lost for good, she finds a way to dive into it and live it...with monumental success.

It wasn't too late for Sara to follow her dreams and it's never too late for you to follow yours...even the ones you thought you had given up.

It's never too late to rekindle the hope that has shriveled into hopelessness. And it's never too early to give up on the idea of giving up!

My Story

It's August 2013, a few weeks before my fifty-ninth birthday, and I have just completed a first draft of my stage-musical adaptation of *The SunQuest,* third story in my *Q'ntana* fantasy series. I have been at this nonstop for eight weeks now. I began by adapting *The MoonQuest,* the first story, and continued straight through with *The StarQuest* and *The SunQuest.* I'm beyond burnt out.

For more than twenty-five years, I have treated writing as a spiritual pursuit, writing from the deepest inner places I have been able to access. It's also what I've taught. But on this day, I feel as though I have sacrificed too much for too little: My book sales are poor, my coaching income is negligible, I no longer have a home or car of my own and the emotional pain of digging so deep has grown unbearable.

On this day, I declare to my closest friends that I'm on strike. "If I'm going to return to writing," I insist, "something has to shift. Otherwise, I'm giving it up. The work is much too hard for so pitiful a payoff."

My friends, some of whom are writers themselves, make sympathetic noises. I'm certain that they don't doubt my sincerity, but I suspect they doubt my determination. "Let them doubt," I mutter as I settle into a diet of Netflix and murder mysteries. "If nothing changes, I'm not going back."

I make one modest concession: I commit to editing and posting a "pre-strike" interview I had conducted with *New York Times* bestselling mystery author J.A. Jance.

About thirty minutes into our recorded conversation, as we're chatting about craft, I tell Jance how much I love that she never outlines her books because I don't either.

"I have to sort of step out with faith," she says, "that if I can write the first sentence of the book, I can eventually get to the end of it."

"Shit," I exclaim to the recording. The moment Jance talks about the faith that carries her from her first sentence to her last, I know that my strike is over. My creative and spiritual lives have always been inextricably linked, and both have been built on a solid foundation of faith.

As Jance's words echo in my heart and mind, I realize that if the deepest part of me has determined that I am a writer and that my writing (and all that derives from it) is the most important part of my being, I can't walk away from it. I can't give up. I can't abandon my faith and I can't stop surrendering to it.

I am a writer. Period.

The Way of the Fool

It's simple. The Fool never gives in and the Fool never gives up. He does not let setbacks overwhelm him. She does not let roadblocks discourage her. He recognizes that what appears on the surface to be a setback is nothing more than a nudge in a new, more perfect direction. She recognizes that a roadblock is always an opportunity, never a barrier; always an opening, never a shutting down.

The Fool knows that every road he is called to take is the right road, even if it is not the road he set out on. The Fool knows too that every right road can only be followed to its ending, wherever that takes her and however it carries her there. The Fool also knows that endings don't matter because every ending is but a new beginning.

Because there are no endings only new beginnings along this path, there is no abandoning it and there is no turning back. It would be pointless. Even as the Way of the Fool is rarely a direct path, it is always a forward-moving one, an upward-moving one.

The Way of the Fool is the way of commitment. The Way of the Fool is the way of new beginnings and fresh starts.

A Fool-ish Story

Author Madeleine L'Engle received two years' worth of rejections from twenty-six publishers for her novel *A Wrinkle in Time*, which, once it was finally published in 1962, went on to win major awards and be translated into more than a dozen languages. It's still popular and is now considered a classic.

Toward the end of that demoralizing two-year period, L'Engle covered up her typewriter and decided to give up, on *A Wrinkle in Time* and on writing. Moments later L'Engle had an idea for a new novel — about failure. In a flash, she was back at her typewriter.

"That night," as she explained thirty years later in a PBS documentary, "I wrote in my journal, 'I'm a writer. That's who I am. That's what I am. That's what I have to do — even if I'm never, ever published again.' And I had to take seriously the fact that I might never, ever be published again. ... It's easy to say I'm a writer now, but I said it when it was hard to say. And I meant it."

Your Story

Ask Yourself These Questions…

Ask yourself these questions in your *Way of the Fool* journal but don't think about the answers. And don't feel you have to answer each question individually if that doesn't feel right.

Let your individual answers (or whatever single answer these questions trigger) emerge freely and honestly, writing them on the Muse Stream in a free-flowing, stream-of-consciousness way where appropriate.

- Are there dreams (or other things in your life) that you've already given up on? What are they? Describe them as fully as you can. Why did you let them go?

- How do those dreams feel to you today? Be honest: Whether or not you believe them to be attainable, do they remain desirable to you in some way? In what way? If they are no longer desirable the way you first envisioned them, would some minor or major adjustment render them desirable to you again?

- Now, take a still-desirable dream that you abandoned and view it again from where you are now, as who you are now. Again be honest: Is there any part of it that you can find a way to rekindle and begin to live? Is there any part of it that you can alter or adapt to make it more possible in your life today? What one step can you take today, *right now*, to begin to bring that dream back to life, in your life?

Exploration

There's a scene in *Star Trek: The Next Generation* where Jean-Luc Picard is presented with a sculpture of a humanoid. When he lifts off the removable top of the art piece, more than a dozen identical beings are nested inside it. Like that sculpture, we carry within us many facets and aspects that make up the greater whole that we view as Self.

If you're feeling as though you want to give up on something in your life — on your dreams, perhaps, like I did with writing — it can be helpful to identify and connect with that part of you that wants to walk away or otherwise block your forward movement.

How? It's not as hard as it might sound. First, let me tell you a story...

Some years back, I woke up nauseous and sweating from a nightmare. In the dream I was trying to walk out of an underground parking garage but the uniformed attendant refused to let me pass. I argued. He argued back. I shouted. He shouted back. Whatever I said or did was met with unyielding resistance.

A few days later I decided to try to reproduce the dream in meditation to see if I could alter the outcome. I called the surly guard back into my consciousness and he again refused me passage. This time, instead of arguing with him, I calmly asked him why. Over the course of our conversation, he revealed to me that his job was to protect me. "If I let you leave here," he argued, "I will be out of work."

For a moment, I was startled by the disclosure. Then, from some deep well of inner wisdom, I reassured him that I continued to need his protection, but in new ways. With that, he agreed to learn to act more as a filter than a block, we embraced, and I strode past him and out into the sunlight, having turned a barrier to my forward movement into a willing and eager helper.

Now It's Your Turn...

As you have done with all the meditative experiences in *The Way of the Fool*, use your breath to get into a relaxed, contemplative space. If you're still feeling tense, run slowly up through your body — from your toes to the top of your head — breathing consciously into any areas that feel particularly stressed.

Then, gently and with love, invite the part of yourself that wants to give up on something in your life — or already has — to sit down with you. You can do this silently with your eyes closed, or you can write the conversation down as it's happening, as I did with my parking attendant. Regardless, do it in a free-flowing, Muse Stream way and do your best to not think about what's going on and to remain compassionate and free of judgment.

Start by asking that part of you to identify itself and to explain why it feels the way it does...why it is ready to give up. This is not about eliminating, expelling or killing off any part of you. That would be an unhealthy and self-destructive way of going about this. Rather, it's about finding out what sparked your sense of hopelessness.

Perhaps, as with my parking attendant, that part of you wants to give up out of fear. Perhaps it is trying to protect the rest of you from something. Or perhaps it has its own reason, one that is unique to your situation. Whatever is revealed to you through this process, begin by offering reassurance to that part of you and then invite it to explore with you how hope might be restored, motivation renewed and forward motion reignited. This may be a negotiation, but remember to keep the powerful, fearless, hopeful and motivated parts of you lovingly in charge.

Use the following questions and/or your own as part of your dialogue and allow the answers to come naturally, whether on the pages of your *Way of the Fool* journal or in your mind's eye. Don't force the answers. Don't judge or censor. Remember to go with first thoughts. Remember to breathe.

- Who are you?
- Do you have a name?
- Why do you want to give up on *xxx*? Or, why did you give up on xxx?
- Why don't/didn't you want me more forward with *xxx*?
- What are/were you afraid of?
- Why are/were you feeling hopeless and/or helpless?
- What can I do to reassure you?
- What would make you feel safer? More hopeful? More motivated?
- How can I "retrain" you so that we can work together and no longer be at odds?

Don't be discouraged if you don't get all the answers you seek in a single session. There's a good chance that you won't. If that happens, rejoin the conversation again another day, and another, if necessary. And if you still feel like giving up after having a dialogue with one part of yourself, call in another and repeat the experience.

My Story: Coda

I would be lying if I said that I never again doubted and that I never again half-wished that I could turn my back on the sometimes-onerous demands of my Muse. But every time I have been tempted, I do my best to remember my writer's strike and the words of faith that aborted it. Over the years I have come to realize that once you step onto the Way of the Fool, there is no way off that isn't soul-destroying. There's a reason why my memoir titled itself *Acts of Surrender*: The Way of the Fool *is* the way of surrender.

Affirmation

I, *your full name*, tap into the infinite well of hope that lies within me and commit to the Fool that I am, who is never without hope. And so it is.

Step #10. Embrace the Mystery

"Nothing here makes any sense!"
THE STARQUEST

It's human nature to want to understand, to want to figure out, to want to know. Some of our greatest scientific discoveries have come from that innate curiosity about how the world works.

Yet there is a difference between "wanting to know," which derives from a healthy spirit of inquiry, and "needing to know," which too often demonstrates a lack of trust.

When we are fixated on a "need" to know, what we are truly doing is craving control. "If I know what's going on and why it's going on, everything will make sense, I will be in control and I will be safe."

Yet some of our most transformative advances and profound breakthroughs have occurred when an absolute need for certainty is abandoned in favor of the freedom of open-ended exploration…when we turn away from the common sense of the well-trodden path and step into the uncommon wisdom of the road less traveled...when we stop asking "why" (and insist on an answer that makes sense) and start asking "what if"?

What if we could stop insisting that our world make sense to our logical minds? What if we could surrender instead to "heart sense"? What if we could give up the *need* to know without losing our natural inquisitiveness? What if we could abandon control? What if, like the Fool, we could leap in faith?

What if?

My Story

WHEN I DROVE OUT of Sedona in the wake of my failed marriage, I figured I would wander around for a few months until my heart sent me to a new home — much like it had when I'd left Toronto eight years earlier. Instead, nearly three years had passed and I was still on the road. I'd crossed America four times and whenever I landed in a new town, I wondered whether this was where my endless-seeming journey would finally come to an end. "Is this my new home?" I would always ask. It never was.

Ironically, I had never asked the question about Albuquerque. Or maybe it's simply that I'd grown tired of sensing no answer when I did, despite the fact that I had spent more time in that city than in any other single place.

Now, I was back there again, having checked into my regular room at the Howard Johnson Express with no clear plan for the next days or weeks.

It was a few minutes past seven on my first morning there when my room phone rang.

"Mr. Gerson?"

"Yes?" I croaked through my bleary-eyed fog. I have never woken up easily or quickly.

"You'd better come to the front desk."

"What?"

"Someone broke into your car. The police are here."

Some things speed the wake-up process. This was one of them. Moments later, I was dressed and in the lobby.

A guest at the hotel next door had called 9-1-1 and

by the time the police arrived, the culprits had fled — fortunately, with nothing of real value: some personal documents, my point-and-shoot camera and the digital audio recorder I had used to record my now-suspended teleconference events. Not sophisticated enough to recognize the marketability of my Canadian passport, they had left it on the front passenger seat.

As I filled out police reports and called banks, credit card issuers, insurance companies and auto-glass outlets, I struggled to parse some higher significance from something that seemed so random and meaningless. After thirty-three months of journeying without a single incident or concern, why now? Why here?

By the end of the day I had intuited an answer: My itinerant days had come to an end. It was not an answer that bore any common sense connection to the break-in, yet I knew in my heart that it was the right one.

I had finally landed. Even if the logic of the message eluded me, even if the "why" was shrouded in mystery, Albuquerque was to be my new home.

The Way of the Fool

The Fool leaps into the unknown. She cannot know what awaits her at the bottom of the cliff. Perhaps it has no bottom and she will fall forever. He cannot know if he will ever reach the bottom of the cliff. Perhaps his sleeve will snag on a jutting branch and he will hang suspended over the valley, savoring the view. Perhaps she will drop only a few feet onto a protruding ledge. Perhaps an eagle will pluck him out of the sky. Perhaps some supernatural force will intervene and transport her to another location…or universe…or dimension.

More likely than any of those is an outcome he cannot conceive, for the greatest gifts are those we cannot imagine.

If the Fool is destined for some unimaginable fate, why bother trying to imagine it? Why not simply enjoy the journey, wherever it carries him and however it carries him there? Why bother asking who or where or how or when or why or whether? Why not simply surrender to the mystery?

When you relish the unknowable and leap willingly into the unknown, you walk the Way of the Fool.

A Fool-ish Story

Everyone thought that Anand Kesavan was crazy when he walked away from his high-paying job in 2008. But the twenty-seven-year-old investment banker was overworked, overstressed and overweight. Simply put, his high-powered job and upper-class lifestyle were slowly killing him.

"I took a leave of absence, sold all of my belongings and traveled the world for eighteen months," he told *Forbes* in 2015. Among the highlights of his journeyings were his time at a community school in Guatemala and helping to raise funds for another school in India. Both experiences "made me realize that money isn't the true measure of success" and both paved the way for a radical career change…and a radical pay cut: He became chief financial officer at a Texas charter school for kids in underserved populations.

Today, Kesavan is founder and CEO of Charter Impact Fund, a nonprofit fund that helps high-performing, high-impact charter schools maximize their resources for students. It's more than a job; it's a calling, and one that marries Anand Kesavan's original career with the commitment to social justice he discovered on his Fool-ish, "embrace the mystery" world tour.

Your Story

Exploration • I

Years ago, before there were smartphones or even an internet, I booked a trip to Europe, knowing only my initial destination and the date and airport of my final departure. I traveled light, with no checked bags, and I had nothing to guide me other than a Eurailpass, a few guidebooks and the maps and train schedules I picked up along the way. For six weeks I wandered from city to city and country to country, following my intuition and the voice of my heart — even though at the time I had no conscious awareness of either.

Novelist E.L. Doctorow once noted that writing is like driving at night in the fog. "You can only see as far as your headlights," he said, "but you can make the whole trip that way." My European trip was much like that, and it was filled with the unexpected encounters, amazing discoveries and extraordinary experiences that always show up for us when we abandon control and embrace the mystery.

Try This

Have you ever started your car and simply taken off, with no clear itinerary and no fixed destination? Have you ever gone for an aimless walk, just to see where your feet would carry you? Have you ever boarded a bus, subway or commuter train with no plan other than to enjoy the ride, wherever it takes you? Now is the time to try any or all of those experiences.

Turn off your cellphone and, if you're driving, your

vehicle's GPS and take off. Walk, drive, take public transit or mix 'n match your modes of transportation. Give yourself a full morning or afternoon or, if you can spare it, a full day. Stop somewhere you've never been for coffee or a meal. Strike up a conversation with a stranger. Pop into a store or a park or a museum or some other site of conventional or unconventional interest along the way, preferably a place you're visiting for the first time. And do your best to not return along the same route.

When you get back, write about your experiences in your *Way of the Fool* journal. Where did you go? What did you see? What did you discover? What was fun? What was less fun? Who did you talk to and what did you talk about? Then, continuing in your journal, explore what it would feel like if you gave yourself permission to do more of that in your everyday life.

Try This Too
If you commute regularly to work, alter your route or mode of transport or both. Is there someplace you regularly shop? Shop somewhere else instead, maybe in a different part of town. Do you have a regular coffee hangout? Try somewhere new, maybe in a neighborhood you don't know, and change your regular drink for something you've never tried before.

What else can you do today to break those regular patterns that are keeping you rutted in routine? Whatever it is, do it. Now.

Exploration • II

When I was writing my first novel, *The MoonQuest*, I rarely knew from one day to the next — sometimes, from one sentence to the next — where the story would take me. It was an often-stressful challenge to all the ways I had tried to maintain some semblance of control over my life.

Whenever the story tried to fly off in a direction that appeared to make no sense, I longed to rein it in. Yet every time I let it, every time I surrendered to the seeming senselessness and embraced the mystery, the story proved itself to be wiser, more creative and more compelling than anything my controlling mind could ever have conceived.

Explore your answers to the following questions in your *Way of the Fool* journal…

- Where in your life have you surrendered to the seemingly senseless and embraced the mystery? Where did it take you? What were the consequences?

- Where in your life were you given that opportunity but passed it by? What did you miss out on experiencing?

- Where in your life do you now have that opportunity? What choice are you leaning toward making?

- Can you let yourself abandon control enough to surrender to something your logical mind can't quite grasp? What would be involved? What first step can you take today, *right now*?

My Story: Coda

I would end up living in Albuquerque off and on for ten years, longer than in any other place I had called home since leaving Toronto in 1994 for Nova Scotia.

Here, I would establish my persona as an author and screenwriter: I landed in Albuquerque with one just-published book, one about-to-be published book, two incomplete manuscripts and one incomplete screenplay. By the time I left I had completed four screenplays, three of which had been optioned; and I had published fifteen books and started on a sixteenth.

Here, I would also establish my identity as a workshop facilitator and creativity coach: If most of my clients were based elsewhere, it was in Albuquerque that I crafted most of my course material and shaped much of my approach to coaching.

Looking back, my time in Albuquerque was about building foundations. Yet I couldn't know that when a seemingly senseless break-in prompted me to break out of my itinerant way of life and put down roots. They didn't end up being deep roots. But they were deep enough to keep me there…until it was time to leave.

Affirmation

I, *your full name*, give up my need to know, surrender to the mystery and allow myself to be guided in faith as the Fool that I am. And so it is.

Step #11. Embrace the Magic

*"Once you let yourself dream the impossible,
the impossible will come to pass."*
THE MOONQUEST

Miracles are at hand in every moment of every day.

It's our limited vision that prevents us from seeing them. It's our limited sense of what is possible that prevents us from believing in them. It's our fear that prevents us from embracing them.

How do we attract more magic and more miracles into our lives?

By opening our eyes, hearts and minds in awe and gratitude to the abundant miracles already magically present — from the miracles of breath, of laughter, of love, of life, to the magic of a flower, a rainbow, a seascape, a sunrise, to the miracles of serendipity, synchronicity, wonder, connection.

It's not about "expecting" miracles to show up. Expectation takes us out of the now moment.

Rather, it's about acknowledging what is already abundantly present in our field of vision, for it is our openness to everyday miracles that seeds the exceptional ones.

And it is the exceptional ones that remind us that on the Way of the Fool, the impossible is always possible.

My Story

THE CALL WAS CLEAR. After ten years in and out of New Mexico and more than twenty years spent largely in desert climes, it was time for a change. It was time to leave the stark, monastic beauty of the Southwest for the lush luxuriance of the Pacific Northwest. It was time to take my greatest leap of faith yet: a 1,500-mile leap to a city I didn't know, a leap without the safety net of savings, prospects, friends or family.

Like the Fool, I have leapt off many cliffs over the years, if never as fearlessly as the Fool manages. At the same time I have always done my best to embrace the magic and, like the Fool, I have always been blessed with miracles. My planned move to Portland was no exception.

The first miracle showed up even before I decided to leave Albuquerque: I woke up one morning feeling that it was time to *consider* getting a new car. My then-existing vehicle, itself a miracle, was seventeen years old and, although in reasonably good running order, was requiring more and more repairs to keep it that way.

I arranged to visit a Toyota dealership later that afternoon to explore my options; I left four hours later in a new 2017 Prius that I didn't expect to be able to afford. When, little over a month later, I heard Portland's call, I was able to answer it knowing I had a car that could safely make the journey.

But where would I land, and how would I pay for my move and the start of a new life?

Within weeks of having made my decision to leave, a friend pressed a check into my hands. She had made her own leap-of-faith move some years earlier and had been helped in similar fashion. That was the next miracle.

Soon after, I set my departure date. Yet I still didn't know where I was going to land. Would I have to stay in a hotel at the other end while I figured out what to do and where to do it? And what would I do with my belongings? I didn't have much, but it wouldn't all fit in the Prius. And once in Portland, would it all have to go into storage while I sorted myself out?

Before I could seriously address those questions, there was a third miracle…or at least the possibility of one: Out of the blue it looked as though I might finally be paid for three screenplays that had been optioned several years back. Were that to happen, I could easily launch a new life in Portland.

That was the good news. The less-than-good news was that the money would not likely be paid until late winter or early spring. In the meantime I would need to figure out what to do with myself and my stuff.

Then another miracle showed up: an offer of a months' housesitting in Portland's lushly sylvan Maplewood neighborhood. Of course, I accepted.

And a further miracle: What happened when the month was up, the screenplay money was delayed and I lacked the finances to rent an apartment of my own? The people I was housesitting for invited me to rent my room and stay on.

One miracle after the next after the next…each fueled by some action on my part:

- I had to decide to go look at cars, even though I was certain I couldn't afford a new one.

- I had to decide I was going to move to Portland, even without the visible means to do it.
- I had to commit to a moving date, even though I had no place to land.

In short, I had to believe in the existence of miracles and know that if I let go and trusted enough to leap, my faith would keep me safe.

It did.

The Way of the Fool

The Fool is the epitome of magic and miracle. Any life lived on the other side of convention and conventional logic always is.

At the same time the Fool neither views miracles as remarkable nor magic as unusual. The Fool views them as the everyday, every-breath occurrences they truly are. After all, magic and miracle infuse everyone and everything. Even that which others might consider ordinary carries within it some element of the extraordinary in the Fool's eyes. Even those whom others might dismiss as bland and colorless carry a glint of fire and a spark of brilliance in the Fool's heart. How could they not when life itself is magical and all existence is a miracle?

As the Fool steps off his cliff, he does not expect some supernatural force to save him. In the childlike innocence of her moment-to-moment existence, there can be no expectation, for nothing exists beyond the always-mystical now. Besides, the Fool knows that the next moment will carry at least as many miracles as does this one…so why even think about it?

When you acknowledge magic's power in your life, you walk a path that is abounding in miracles. You walk the Way of the Fool.

A Fool-ish Story

Toward the end of my fantasy novel *The MoonQuest*, the four protagonists are spared from drowning by a miracle: When they hold hands, with a mystical stone sandwiched between each pair of palms, the ocean's surface magically supports them.

Unfortunately, in order to move forward on their quest, they must toss the stones into the sea. The problem is that once they unlink hands, the magic that supports them will vanish.

They have two choices: They can stay safe but immobilized, or they can trust in the existence of an even greater miracle than the one that has kept them from drowning.

Fearfully, they trust enough to let go…and start to sink. Was this a mistake? Did the voice of their hearts steer them wrong? It sure looks that way. But as the water swallows them up and it seems certain they will drown, that "greater miracle" manifests and they are magically transported to where they need to be.

Miracles are forged from a kind of alchemy: We listen for the voice of our heart and act accordingly — in faith. Our action is not impulsive, nor is it driven by panic. And it's rarely logical. It's the Way of the Fool.

Your Story

Exploration

As I write this (or, rather, dictate it into my phone), I am sitting at a picnic table overlooking the Willamette River in South Portland. It's a glorious spring day, not too hot, with a cool breeze whispering at me through the trees. The river is sparkling with reflected sunlight. I'm surrounded by the lushness of spring-awakened verdure. And despite the low rumble of city sound, the air is alive with birdsong.

I could fill a whole book with the magic and miracle of this moment. Perhaps the most dramatic miracle for me is the fact that I'm in Portland at all, that I answered the call to come here entirely on faith and that I find myself falling in love with a city I had never before visited…unless you count a stopover of a few hours more than a decade ago.

What about you? If magic and miracles are everyday occurrences, existing around us regardless of where we are or what we're doing, then you too are surrounded by magic and miracles *right now*, even if you're not sitting in a place of natural beauty.

Take a moment to look around you. What do you see? Whatever it is, can you see the magic in it? Can you find the miracle in it?

Keep looking, keep feeling, keep experiencing, keep acknowledging. What do you see now? Can you find the wonder in it? Your awe for it?

Now, cast your mind back over your day. Where were you? What were you doing? What were you feeling? Where were you courageous? Who were you interacting with?

Within those experiences and feelings lie much magic and many miracles, if you are prepared to open your heart and mind to them…if you are prepared to acknowledge them.

What about elsewhere in your life? What about the larger miracles? We have all experienced some of those. What about your current situation? Are you sitting at home? In a library or café? Are you at work? On a bus, streetcar, commuter train or subway? On an airplane? On vacation?

Your home itself is a miracle, and not simply that you are in it (perhaps there are miracle/magic stories there); it's a miracle of architecture, engineering and workmanship.

Think of the miracle of creativity that produced all those library books. And don't forget the publishing magic that got them onto all those library shelves.

Are you in your dream job? That has got to be some sort of miracle. Or do you hate or barely tolerate your job? Or are you unemployed? If your work/professional life isn't satisfying — or is nonexistent — can you focus on the magic elsewhere in your life? However inconsequential it appears to your mind to be, it *is* significant. Training your awareness on it will always help kindle fresh miracles in your life, perhaps even in your work/professional world.

Don't forget your health. Even if you're facing health challenges, your health is itself a miracle. You're alive, right? The breath that gives you life is a profound miracle, as is any medical assistance that helps makes that breath possible.

The list of possibilities is infinite! Think of the miracle of growth when you plant a seed. Think of the magic that converts raw ingredients into a gourmet meal or a luscious dessert. Think of the miracle of those raw ingredients themselves and the magic that transported them from farm or field to you. Think of the distance traveled by the coffee beans that transformed berries on a tree to the morning elixir that started your day…or the miracle of the tea leaves if you're a tea drinker.

Let your awareness continue to expand and become more and more conscious of the magic in your life, of the miracles in your life. Be in wonder. Be awestruck. Be grateful. Not only for the purposes of this exercise, but as you move forward in your day and in the days ahead.

Try This in Your "Way of the Fool" Journal
Before you go to bed tonight, jot down ten miracles or examples of magic that you experienced in your life today. They needn't be massive or life-altering. Remember that everyday miracles can be even more significant than the fireworks-generating variety because those are the ones we tend to overlook.

Maintain this nightly inventory for two weeks and notice how every day's entry is easier to make. Notice too how many more examples of magic and miracle you have to choose from each evening as you make your entries.

My Story: Coda • I

After three months in the house in Maplewood — one as a house sitter and two as a month-to-month renter — I knew it was time to move on. As welcome as the miracle had been that installed me there, my living situation was not the vision I'd had for myself in coming to Portland.

It was more than that: All my inner guidance was urging me to take a new leap of faith, to once again commit to leaving one place with no idea where I would go next or how I would find the resources to get there (Step #7).

I already knew where I wanted to live: in a brand-new building in the downtown Pearl District. But it was beyond my means. Frankly, not much was within my means… apart from the room I had just announced I was vacating. Still, I recognized that the fire of magic always requires the kindling of action — action that's grounded in faith. So like the Fool I have so often been, I leapt.

As I write these words, I have not yet landed. Yet a leap of faith is just that: a leap of *faith*. Without knowing what my next miracle will look like, I know that it is only a breath away from making its magical presence known. I know too that its ultimate expression will surpass anything I could consciously imagine. Meantime, and not always easily and not always comfortably, I trust.

My Story: Coda • II

Some miracles have a short shelf life, if only so they can be superseded by even more powerful magic. That was true for the characters in the *MoonQuest* story I just shared, and it has once again proven to be true for me. Within weeks of my leap of faith, I learned that the money for my trio of screenplays was about to be released. My long-awaited payment was within sight and, with it, the new life in Portland that I had envisioned.

I wrote the preceding paragraph a few weeks before I learned that the screenplay money would finally be coming my way. Writing the story as I desired for it to unfold was part of the alchemy that created the miracle. More about that when we get to Step 12½.

Affirmation

I, *your full name*, choose to be more aware, more in wonder and more in awe of the abundant miracles that are always present in my life. I embrace the magic as the Fool that I am. And so it is.

Step #12. Remember Who You Are

"You are a being of such immense power that were you able see it fully, you might not believe it was you. It is."
THE BOOK OF MESSAGES:
WRITINGS INSPIRED BY MELCHIZEDEK

Who are you? You are more than a mass of skin, bone, muscle and sinew. More than the blood pumping through your heart and coursing through your veins. More than the breath that flows into your lungs and out again. More than all the cells that unite to shape your physical body.

You are more than your brain's incomparable power to reason, compute, calculate and recall. More than its immeasurable ability to amass, assess, organize and analyze.

You are stronger than the most muscular of machines, more resilient than the most elastic of rubbers, more powerful than the most formidable of turbines.

You are greater than the sum of your emotions. Greater, certainly, than your fear. You are passion and compassion. You are generosity and benevolence. You are boundless courage. You are love without limit. You are a miracle of heart and soul.

You are the Infinite expressing itself in finite form. You are divine perfection living as the perfect expression of human imperfection.

You are a human being who too easily forgets all that. So take a moment to remember who you are!

My Story

IT'S EARLY — WAY TOO EARLY — on a Monday morning, and I'm driving to Oregon Health Sciences University for an MRI. Until this moment, I haven't been overly concerned about the test or about its possible results. But it's easy, when you're tired, hungry, uncaffeinated and on your way to a consequential cancer screening, to question your mortality.

Within an hour, however, my mortality no longer matters, my earlier concerns washed away in the flood of hopelessness and futility that overpowers me during the MRI's thirty-five minutes of relentlessly unbearable discomfort. As I lie motionless (I'm not allowed to move) in the noisy enclosure (even with earplugs and headphones, the sound is deafening), all I can do is compare what I'm feeling physically with the profound emotional discomfort of my thirty-five year Fool's journey. The parallels are disturbing, distressing and depressing. And by the time I drive off the OHSU campus, that journey feels as though it has been more foolish than Fool-ish, and I can't help but wonder what the point of it all has been.

"I have spent the past decades doing my best to not repeat my mother's mistakes," I text a friend later that day, "and to live from a place of following my heart, not from a place of fear. I don't want to come to the end of my life filled with so many regrets that, like her, I just give up. But here I am, wondering, like her, if it's not that I was screwed over but that I screwed it all up."

It has always seemed to me that my mother welcomed her cancer diagnosis as a way to escape a lifetime of regretted choices. If my MRI were to find a tumor, I don't want to do likewise. Yet I think I now understand how she might have felt.

I stumble numbly through the next fifty hours in a fog of despair and self-pity, wondering what I will say in three weeks when I step onto the platform to deliver an inspirational talk at New Thought Center for Spiritual Living, let alone in three days when I am to lunch with my friend Isa who is in town to explore her own spiritually inspired move to Oregon. This is the same friend who two weeks earlier said to me, "You're the bravest person I know." I feel like a fraud.

I have experienced other crises of faith over the years but none this profound, none this intense. I wonder if I will ever see the other side of it.

It is now Thursday morning and I'm on my way to meet Isa for lunch, still unsure what I will say to her. I glance at the clock. It's 11:11.

It has been years since I have paid serious attention to the 11:11's and 12:12's that show up in my life. But when I see it now, I instantly recall a powerful dream from the night before.

In the dream, it's 11:11 on November 11, Remembrance Day in my native Canada, and I suddenly remember that I forgot to pause for the traditional moment of silent remembrance.

The dream, I realize, is a call to remember who I am: not the Mark David Gerson who is flailing in despair, but a powerful being of light, a courageous journeyer traveling the Way of the Fool.

The Way of the Fool

The Fool knows he is a Fool, and with a Fool's wisdom, he knows that there is nothing else he needs to know. Nor is there anything she needs to remember. When you know nothing, there can be nothing to forget.

The Fool spends no time thinking about who or what he is. The Fool simply is. He moves from one moment's existence to the next, fully himself in each new breath. When you are fully yourself in each new breath, there is no need to remember who you were in a previous breath.

The Fool never contemplates her self-worth or compares herself with anyone or anything else. The Fool views each being, including himself, as the perfect expression in each moment of his divine essence and soul's imperative. When you view yourself in each moment as the perfect expression of your divine essence and soul's imperative, there is nothing to forget and thus nothing to remember.

In the instant before he was transformed into a Fool, the Fool remembered one final time who he was, in all his wholeness and holiness. In the next instant, when she stepped into the fullness and foolness of her Fool-ishness, there was nothing more to remember. For never again was there any more forgetting.

A Fool-ish Story

Lucy Stone remembered who she was: She was Lucy *Stone*, not Lucy Blackwell, not even Lucy Stone Blackwell.

Born in rural Massachusetts in 1818, Stone was already a leading abolitionist and suffragist when she married fellow activist Henry Blackwell in 1855.

Initially, she took Blackwell's name, as was the custom. But a year later, declaring that "a wife should no more take her husband's name than he should hers" and after having been assured by Salmon P. Chase, a prominent lawyer and family friend (who would later be named Chief Justice of the Supreme Court) that there was no law requiring a married woman to adopt her husband's name, she reverted to her birth name, becoming the first American woman to retain her maiden name for her entire life.

Your Story

Meditation: Remember Who You Are

Have your Way of the Fool *journal handy to record your thoughts, feelings and impressions. Allow at least 30 minutes for this meditative/journaling experience.*

Close your eyes, settle back into whatever you're sitting on or lying on, and take a deep breath. As you breathe in, breathe in the stillness of this moment. And as you breathe out, breathe out all the stresses and strains that preceded this moment. Breathe in sweet surrender, and breathe out everything about this day that has caused you worry, anxiety, anger, fear or despair. Breathe in the lightness that is your natural state, and breathe out any heaviness that in this moment and in any way weighs you down.

You are a wondrous and wonder-filled being of passion, light and love…a transcendent expression of the Divine in human form. Breathe into that, into a knowingness of that, into a whole-body, whole-mind, wholehearted certainty of that. Breathe out *anything* that does not align with that representation of your truth, with that truth of your beingness.

Breathe in the power and empowerment you are. Breathe in your unlimited power to soar, to glide, to fly, to be free. To see. Breathe in the vast power of your vision. The boundless power of your spirit. The immeasurable power of your soul.

Breathe in the healing, the forgiveness, the compassion, the gratitude and the hope that you are. The wholeness and holiness that you are. The infinite wisdom that you are. Breathe out all that prevents you from acknowledging it, that holds you back from experiencing it, that denies you the ability to make it manifest in your life.

You are the ideal expression in this lifetime of the divine spark that is your essence, a divine spark that is waiting to ignite within you as the full potential of the human story that you have been called here to live, to be.

Only you can live that story, and live it you must, regardless of the voices, inner and outer, that cry out for you to stop, that insist that they are trying to save you — from ridicule, from judgment, from shame.

There can be no salvation in stopping, in turning away, in listening to those voices — however sensible they might in the moment seem. Your only salvation is the step that must emerge from the prison of your fear and into the light of your potential as you remember who and what you are, the fullness of who and what you are. As you remember with this breath, and now this one. And now this one.

One breath following the next and the next, crashing through what you think you know — about yourself and the world — and carrying you into the Kingdom of the New, that wondrous realm beyond your imagining that has been waiting for you since the dawn of time.

Waiting for you to remember it. Waiting for you to be it. Waiting for you to be. Waiting for you to take that next step on the Way of the Fool that has called you to it.

Commit to that next step, whatever it is that emerges in your sacred remembering. Take that step, in the courage and humility of your journey, of your path. Open your eyes in full remembering of who you are, and take that step.

My Story: Coda

Even after recalling and interpreting my 11:11 dream, it took thirty-six hours of reaffirming "I remember who I am" before I felt my faith had been restored, before I felt that I might have something to offer the congregation at New Thought Center for Spiritual Living. It was then that the next gift of my existential crisis materialized: this book.

I had already titled my talk "The Way of the Fool," although I hadn't yet given much thought to its content. Now "The Way of the Fool" would also be a book.

By the next afternoon, I knew exactly how *The Way of the Fool* would come together, from its 12½ steps to the structure of each step. It was the first time in my writing life that a book idea had come to me fully formed. I jotted down a few quick notes and began to write.

The more I wrote, the more I realized that I was writing *The Way of the Fool* at least as much for me as for you, that I was charting a road map to help get me through a challenging time, that I was crafting a template that would help me realize my dream, that I was forging an eloquent and ongoing reminder of who, at my core, I am.

Affirmation

I, *your full name*, remember who I am. I remember that I am a powerful being of passion, light and love, a transcendent expression of the Divine in human form walking the Way of the Fool. I am that. And I am that I am. And so it is.

Step #12 1/2. Fly Free

"Emerge from the cocoon you have woven around yourself and fly free into the world."
DIALOGUES WITH THE DIVINE:
ENCOUNTERS WITH MY WISEST SELF

The Way of the Fool is a voyage of faith. There are no paved roads, worn paths or marked trails. There are only the roads, paths and trails that you yourself blaze. There are no predetermined routes or fixed GPS coordinates. There is only the direction that calls you in this moment…and now in this one.

Yes, it can seem random. But the heart's journey is never random. Yes, it can seem erratic. But the soul's journey is never erratic.

Those perceptions derive from a mind that yearns for control, by a conscious imagination that is limited by what it thinks it knows.

When you let go of that expression of the finite, when you leap off the cliff of certainty into the mysteries of the infinite, that's when you fly. That's when you soar.

That's when you embrace life as the Fool that you are.

My Story

"I'm not who I thought I was!" How many times have I uttered that? I've lost track. There was the slowly dawning realization at age twenty that I was gay. There was the shocking discovery at thirty that the man I had known as my father was not my biological father. There were the creative and spiritual awakenings a few years later that radically altered the trajectory of my life. There was the moment a decade after that when I crossed into the United States from my native Canada and knew I would not be returning. There was the moment ten months later when I unexpectedly fell in love with a woman and, almost immediately, married her. There was the moment less than fifteen months after that when I held my newborn daughter in my arms as the father I never thought I wanted to be.

And there was this morning, when I mailed off my application to become a US citizen. I had been thinking about taking this next step since I got to Portland, but I had always viewed naturalization as nothing more than a convenience: As a dual citizen I would no longer be subject to the restrictions attached to my US green card, including the need to renew it every ten years. I would be free to come and go from the United States as I pleased. I would even be free to live abroad or to return to live in Canada without jeopardizing my US status.

What I didn't realize until I began to fill out the application was that becoming a US citizen was about much more than expedience. It was a dramatic shift in identity. Once again, I'm not who I thought I was.

Every time we shed some fragment of who we *think* we are, we come closer to who we truly are. Every time we slice away one of the beliefs that anchors us to our limited view of ourselves, we rise into a fuller expression of our unlimited potential. Every time we break through the walls that box us in, we know what it is to fly free.

The Way of the Fool

The Fool recognizes no walls, barriers or barricades. The Fool knows no locked doors, bolted gates or impassable fences. The Fool acknowledges no restraints or constraints. The Fool moves freely and effortlessly wherever the moment calls her, however the heart directs him.

The Fool is everyone and everything, all potential and all possibility. The Fool is the heart of all life, the soul of all creation. The Fool is the spirit of sovereignty, the essence of autonomy, the freedom of flight.

Your Story

Meditation: The Butterfly

Have your Way of the Fool *journal handy to jot down your thoughts, feelings and impressions, and allow at least 20 minutes for this meditative/journaling experience.*

My professionally recorded version is available for download or streaming; it's nearly identical to what follows. (Search the relevant site/store for "Mark David Gerson butterfly meditation.")

See "How to Use This Book" for details on how to access the recording, as well as for tips on how best to use all this book's meditations

Close your eyes. Breathe in deeply, fully. Allow your shoulders to drop, and drop some more. And some more. Allow yourself to relax. Fully.

From that place of calm, let your breath transport you into the realm of imagination, the realm of creativity, the realm of vision.

See yourself now in another form, another body. A caterpillar's body.

You're a caterpillar, enfolded in a cocoon. Like a blanket-bundled infant or your blanket-bundled sleep-in self, you're enveloped in the divine caress of in-between time.

In this moment, you're safe. Safe in the all-embracing darkness. Secure in the womb of creation, transformation, rebirth.

Creation. Transformation. Rebirth.

Feel that transformation within you. Feel your shape begin to shift. Feel your body lighten and wings begin to form.

Feel the nascent emergence of color, translucence, delicacy.

Now, feel the pressure of your wings as, pressed between your body and the walls of the cocoon, they begin to push and spread, push and spread. Push and spread.

Such delicate wings, yet so strong. So strong.

Such a delicate body, yet so strong. So strong.

So awake. So determined. So ready.

What was once a sanctuary is now stifling. What once held you in safety now presses against you, holds you down. Holds you back.

Thank the cocoon and the caterpillar you were for letting you sleep, for keeping you safe, for holding you secure. Thank them and release them from the need to do so any longer. Now it's time to awaken.

Now it's time to fly.

Now it's time to be a creature of earth and sky. Of sky and earth. Now it's time to travel great distances, to soar to great heights, to stretch the limits of the possible. To enter into the realm of the improbable, the realm of the impossible.

Feel the walls of your cocoon begin to give way. Feel your wings begin to spread as they push and push and push some more.

It's hard work, at times, to push free of the barriers we have created for ourselves. But we always have the strength. We always have the will. We always have the power.

All we need to do is acknowledge our strength, surrender to our highest imperative and allow our power to have its way with us.

It's time to surrender. To the butterfly you are. To the

creator of your own life that you are. To the free-flowing, free-flying being you are. So do it.

Push one last time with those wings that seem so delicate but carry the strength and will of the universe. Push one last time and feel the walls of your cocoon break apart.

Now, spread your wings to the fullness of their span and fly free.

Fly free.

Fly free.

Now.

You may feel tentative, uncertain. Shaky. That's normal. These are new wings, new experiences, new expressions. Allow the uncertainty, knowing that with each flight you will become more certain, more practiced, more adept.

Fly for as long as you like. Explore your new world from this new perspective. Take your time. And when you're ready to light down again — on a flower petal, on a leaf or on a dew-sparkling blade of grass — open your eyes and your *Way of the Fool* journal and write about your experiences, your feelings, your journey.

Write about them as the caterpillar-turned-butterfly, describing your transformation, your liberation, your flight.

And write about them as the Fool that you are, now free of one more barrier to the freest, fullest expression of your heart's desire.

Exploration • I

It's time to unburden yourself of all that holds you back… of all that walls you in. It's time to let go. It's time to fly! Are you ready to fly? What can you commit to letting go of today, *right now*, to make that take-off more effortless…to not only fly, but to fly high and fly free?

Exploration • II

We have come nearly full circle, from Step #1 to Step #12½, from Break Free to Fly Free, and it's time to complete the cycle. It's time for *you* to write the next chapter of your story. It's time for you to put into writing all that your heart desires, but not as a list of dreams, intentions or wishes. This is not a future-tense story. This a *now* story.

What would it mean for you to fly free? What does your soul yearn for? What would your life look like if you were living your deepest, most heartfelt dreams, right now?

Write that story, in either the present tense as though it is happening in this moment, or in the past tense, as though it has already manifested…whichever feels more natural and true to your voice. Don't write it from your ego mind. Don't write it from your head. Write it from your soul and put your whole heart into it. Don't hold back, and don't leave anything out because it seems impossible. On the Way of the Fool, nothing is impossible. At the same time, not everything shows up precisely as we have ordered it, so be open to variations…especially those that are more magnificent than anything you could have consciously imagined!

Continue to revisit, refine and revise your story as your circumstances, situation and desires shift, and read it regularly — aloud, whenever possible. For extra impact, consider recording it and playing it back in bed as you're falling asleep.

My Story: Coda

I created my own Exploration II story not long after I began to write *The Way of the Fool*, and I was gratified to see how quickly aspects of what I put onto the page began to play out in my life. It helped that I did what I suggested you do: I revised my story as necessary, I read it aloud daily and I recorded it into my phone so that I could listen to it in bed. I can't wait to see what will happen next!

Affirmation

Let the story you wrote in Exploration II be your affirmation. Read it aloud — at least once a day — and watch elements of the story you have written become elements of the story you're living.

Your Story: Coda

Of course, I can no more predict what will change in your life than I can in mine. But if you have committed to what all 12½ steps have asked of you, I know something already has!

The Way of the Fool and You

I'D LOVE TO HEAR about your experiences with *The Way of the Fool* and about any of the ways you are worrying less and loving life more as a result of working with this book's Fool-ish principles.

To that end I have created a dedicated page on my website — www.markdavidgerson.com/yourstories — and I invite you to share your stories and comments there. What you post will remain private and anonymous unless you give me explicit permission to use it, with or without your name.

Share your thoughts and feelings, your stumbles and successes, and your stories. Remember Step #5? Be vulnerable! And if you have questions, feel free to ask them.

While I can't promise to respond to every submission, I will read them all and get back to you wherever possible. I look forward with great anticipation to hearing from you!

Afterword: The Fool and I

IF I WERE TO CHOOSE an archetype to describe my life's journey, it would be the Fool, who is more often than not pictured stepping off a cliff into the unknown. His may be a leap of faith, but it's never blind faith. For the Fool knows that even as she trades the certainty of solid ground for the mysteries of the void, the infinite wisdom of her infinite mind will guide her forward. This knowingness frees him to surrender again and again. And again. Not without resistance and not without fear, but in the conviction that resistance is futile, fear cannot stop her and meaning is always present, even when it is invisible.

The tarot Fool may appear to have a choice in his folly: In many decks, one of his feet is still firmly anchored. He could step back. Or could he? In my favorite representation, from the *Osho Zen Tarot*, it's too late: One foot hangs off the edge; the other only barely touches the earth. She has already leapt.

That's the kind of Fool I am: always in motion, with a momentum that keeps pressing me on to another act of surrender and another…each one pushing me harder than the last…each one nudging me closer to my essential truth…each one requiring a greater leap of faith. And through each, I do my best continue to trust in the Way of the Fool. Its wisdom has never let me down.

Gratitude

I CHOSE NOT TO isolate gratitude as one of the steps on the Way of Fool because every moment in life is one we would do well to be thankful for. The same is true of my experience with this book: I am awed by all it has gifted me, humbled by the priceless treasures it has laid before me and profoundly grateful to all the people, places and experiences, too countless to name, that helped birth it, often unknowingly.

Let's start with the people...

Sander Freedman has been my comrade-in-folly for longer than any friend currently in my life, and my gratitude to him is as boundless as is his courage, wisdom and open heart.

To Joan Cerio, whose life has magically paralleled mine since our paths first crossed in Sedona too many lifetimes-in-this-lifetime ago: Thank you for your unconditional support and abundant sagacity on this Fool-ish journey.

The Way of the Fool might not exist but for Adam Bereki, whose friendship has always been unconditional and unwavering. It was during one of our hours-long conversations that the idea for this book occurred to me.

I would be remiss in not also thanking Kathleen Messmer for her matchless generosity of spirit and Fool-worthy courage.

This is the first book of my now dozen-plus titles not to have some direct link with Albuquerque. It's almost as though *The Way of the Fool* was waiting for me to leave the

Southwest so it could pour itself into me. It is also the first of my books to have arrived fully formed, something that happened only once I arrived in Portland. So I am grateful as well to the energy of my new city — both the verdant oases of its parks and trails and the vibrant bustle of its urban neighborhoods — for inspiring and sustaining this creative enterprise.

I am especially thankful to the score of cafes and their patient baristas for frequently accommodating this eccentric author in his folly. There are too many cafes to list by name, but my most frequented writerly destinations include Sisters Coffee in the Pearl District and Starbucks outlets in Hawthorne, King's Hill, Multnomah Village and Nob Hill.

Finally, to my inner Fool, that part of me that is wiser, freer, more daring and more audacious than the rest of me, thank you — not only for this book but for the journey that made it possible.

The Way of the Fool

Get Your Copies Today!

BE INSPIRED BY MORE OF MARK DAVID'S FOLLY!

Get Your Copies Today!